TRUE **HOCKEY**

THE HABS

BRIAN McFARLANE

PROSPERO
B·O·O·K·S

Library and Archives Canada Cataloguing in Publication
McFarlane, Brian, 1931–
    The Habs/Brian McFarlane.

(True hockey stories)
ISBN 978-1-55267-714-8

Originally publ.: Toronto: Stoddart Publishing Co., 1997
under the title: Brian McFarlane's Original Six: The Habs

    1. Montreal Canadiens (Hockey team) – History. I. Title.
II. Series: McFarlane, Brian, 1931– . True hockey stories.
GV848.M6M33 2008   796.962'640971428   C2008-901735-8

This collection produced for Prospero Books.

Key Porter Books Limited
Six Adelaide Street East, Tenth Floor
Toronto, Ontario
Canada M5C 1H6
www.keyporter.com

Cover design: Alison Carr/Muse Publishing and Communications Inc.
Electronic formatting: Muse Publishing and Communications Inc.
www.musecommunications.ca

Front cover photograph: Henri Richard—Frank Prazak/Hockey Hall of Fame
Printed and bound in Canada.
Printed on environmentally friendly paper using vegetable-based ink.

08 09 10 11 12 5 4 3 2 1

He stood tall on the ice, a peerless superstar resplendent in red, white, and blue. He guided his team to ten Stanley Cups and performed countless heroic deeds with grace and style. To dashing Jean Beliveau, a name synonymous with elegance, élan, and class, a man who always remembered his roots, his family, and his fans, this book is respectfully dedicated.

CONTENTS

CHAPTER 5: **The Toe Blake Era**

CHAPTER 6: **Six Cups in the Seventies**

CHAPTER 7: **Corey and Recent Conflicts**

FOREWORD
by Bob Gainey

When I look back on my NHL hockey career, I realize how very fortunate I was to play 16 seasons with the Montreal Canadiens. When I was drafted by the Canadiens in 1973 from the Peterborough juniors, I was somewhat surprised and even mildly disappointed. Because the Habs had maintained a tradition of excellence over many decades, I knew that opportunities for rookies would be limited. If Sam Pollock expected me to score goals in bunches like Guy Lafleur, Steve Shutt, Jacques Lemaire, or the Mahovlich brothers, he was in for a major disappointment. What's more, I was aware that Montreal rookies had to be patient. Most were shunted off to the Halifax farm team and any lucky enough to stick with the big club spent a lot of time in the press box—learning the game by watching. I was such an unknown on draft day that Ken Dryden later confessed he was confused and wasn't sure whether Sam had selected Bob Gainey or Bob Neely from Peterborough.

I decided that I'd simply report to training camp and give it my best shot. I figured Sam Pollock wouldn't have drafted me eighth overall if he didn't think I had some potential. That summer I got a big break when Rejean Houle and Marc Tardif bolted for the rival WHA. Suddenly there were three or four openings on the Montreal roster. I was told that Scotty Bowman, Montreal's coach at the time, wanted to mix in a couple of solid checkers with his scorers. That was encouraging because checking, not scoring, had always been my forte. Even so, Scotty and Sam decided I should start the season in Halifax, with the Nova Scotia Voyageurs. But I was recalled after just six games and I never went back.

As a professional I worked hard to become a better player. In my second season I found myself on a line with Yvan Cournoyer and Jacques Lemaire, two of the finest pure scorers, and smartest players, in the game. Later I'd team up with Doug Jarvis, another Peterborough grad and a childhood friend, and Jim Roberts. We were assigned to frustrate the other team's top line and we took great pride in our ability to keep some of the NHL's greatest stars off the scoresheet—as much as possible.

The 1975–76 season was an important one for us. In the playoffs that season, we proved that our speed and finesse were more than a match for the intimidating tactics and muscle of the Philadelphia Flyers, two-time Stanley Cup champions. Our confidence soared after our four-game sweep of the Flyers and we went on to three more Stanley Cups in a row. In 1979 I was fortunate enough to win the Conn Smythe Trophy although both Guy Lafleur and Jacques Lemaire scored more points in the playoffs than I did.

It's so satisfying to play on a Cup-winning team. I remember when I first joined the Habs thinking how disappointed I would be if I didn't get a chance to play on a championship team. Guy Lafleur felt the same way. His fear was that the Canadiens had won so many Stanley Cups before his arrival there might not be any left for him to help win.

The four Frank Selke Trophies I won were very meaningful and deeply appreciated because that award brings recognition to the players whose efforts are almost always overshadowed by the more glamorous players— the goal scorers.

To play on a Stanley Cup–winning team is every player's ultimate goal. To play on five is beyond any player's wildest expectations. I often wonder how successful I would have been in hockey, how many frustrations and disappointments I might have encountered, had I been drafted by a team other than the Canadiens.

It's an incredible organization, with more championships than any other team in any other sport. And there's no escaping its rich and fascinating history, its reverence for the men who brought glory to the Canadiens' name. I credit the strength of the Molson family, with a reputation for maintaining an outstanding relationship with employees—keeping them long-term and within a family atmosphere—for much of the Canadiens' success. Such a policy breeds a real sense of loyalty and confidence in those fortunate enough to be on the payroll of such fair-minded people.

I believe most of the teams of the Original Six had good, strong people to lead them, but Montreal seemed to attract a disproportionate number of high-quality individuals who shared a devotion to the game and a deep-rooted desire to succeed in the business of professional hockey.

When the Canadiens celebrated their 75th anniversary back in 1985, a big dinner was held at the Queen Elizabeth Hotel. All the great players from the past got up to speak. There were films of past heroes in their prime. Afterwards, some of the current players sought out those former Habs for their autographs. It was a thrill to be part of it all. One of my teammates—I've forgotten who—once said the Montreal tradition won't carry us. We must carry it.

I know you'll enjoy the fascinating stories about past and present Habs that lie ahead, researched and written by Canada's most prolific hockey author, my longtime friend Brian McFarlane.

Chapter 1
THE EARLY YEARS

How the Canadiens Got Their Name

In researching the Canadiens' famous name, I went back through the records to 1908 and a meeting held, not in Montreal, but in Renfrew, Ontario, a small town in the Ottawa Valley. It seems a Renfrew team, a power in the Upper Ottawa Valley League, a circuit once described as "a fence corner league," wanted a crack at the Stanley Cup. At the meeting it was decided to import star players, offering jobs and other enticements until a Cup challenge from the creamery town could not be ignored. Renfrew's bold hockey ambitions would lead team executive Ambrose O'Brien to another meeting in Montreal one year later. The 1909 meeting would bring together two hockey men who concocted a marvellous idea: create a powerful team of French-speaking hockey players.

By 1909 Renfrew iced a professional team playing in the Federal League against clubs from Cornwall, Smiths Falls, and Ottawa. Goalie Bert Lindsay (father of Ted Lindsay), an import who ran a successful poolroom in town, helped Renfrew win the Federal League championship.

The following season a new league was introduced in Montreal—organizers tabbed it "the greatest league ever formed"—and Renfrew wanted in. Three teams from Montreal were reported to be charter members of the new Canadian Hockey Association: the Nationals, Wanderers, and Shamrocks. Representatives from Quebec and Ottawa, holders of the 1909 Stanley Cup, were invited to join the circuit.

Ambrose O'Brien of Renfrew, then 24, journeyed to Montreal and urged the CHA to consider an application from Renfrew. "Let's make it a six team circuit," he pleaded. "I'll gladly pay the 30 dollars initiation fee you're charging new teams." O'Brien won the support of the Wanderers and the Shamrocks but the Ottawa executives scoffed at his application and persuaded their colleagues to reject the Renfrew bid.

O'Brien left the meeting room quite dejected. But he was not nearly as devastated as Jimmy Gardner, the principal owner of the Wanderers. Gardner emerged from the same meeting at the Windsor Hotel enraged. His team, thought to be a shoo-in for admittance, had just been denied a franchise in the new league. The reason? The other club owners decided the Wanderers' home rink—the Jubilee Arena—was too small so they showed Gardner and his associates the door.

Gardner stomped around the hotel lobby, cursing the men who'd sabotaged his plans. Finally he sat in a chair next to the equally disconsolate O'Brien.

"Ambrose, let's show those arrogant pups a thing or two," he said. "I've got the Wanderers, you've got a good team in Renfrew. And I know you own a couple of teams in Haileybury and Cobalt. Let's start a new league of our own. But we'll need a second team here in Montreal. Why not organize a team of French-speaking players? We'll call it *Les Canadiens*. Who knows? In time such a team could become more popular than any of the other Montreal clubs." And with those words, he laid the foundation for what would become the world's winningest hockey team.

Some historians say that the idea for a team called *Les Canadiens* originated, not with Gardner or O'Brien, but with James Strachan, another part-owner of the Wanderers. But O'Brien, who would put up the money to finance the Montreal franchise, insisted until his death that it was Gardner's idea and Gardner who proposed the name *Les Canadiens*.

In his book *O'Brien*, author Scott Young poses the following question: If the owners of the Wanderers were so sure that a French-Canadian team would be a hit, why did they present it so grandly and free of charge to a 24-year-old from Renfrew? There is a lurking possibility, suggests Young, that it was one of those frequent instances where the progenitors of a great idea prefer to let someone else risk the money to find out if the idea is really so surefire after all.

At any rate, the name *Les Canadiens* appears to have first surfaced during the conversation between Gardner and O'Brien in the lobby of the Windsor Hotel on November 25, 1909.

A week later, on December 2, the new league was formed in Montreal. It was called the National Hockey Association. It was formally agreed to create a new team to be called the *Club de Hockey Canadien*, or *Les Canadiens*.

The next day, on December 3, 1909, after papers were drawn up, the new club became a reality. Financed by wealthy Irish Canadians from Renfrew, and by T. C. Hare of Cobalt, *Les Canadiens* promptly hired Jack Laviolette as manager and first employee. The French-Canadian team was about to take its first tentative skate strides into the world of professional hockey. *Les Canadiens* booked the Jubilee Rink for home games, despite its seating capacity of only 2,700.

Ambrose O'Brien then hired Joe Cattarinich, who, like Laviolette, was a player of note (a goaltender), to help manage *Les Canadiens'* affairs. He signed Newsy Lalonde and Didier Pitre, both flashy goal scorers, to the Canadiens' sparse roster. The public was told that the franchise for the new team would be transferred to a number of Montreal sportsmen or investors as soon as such a group could be put together.

The season opened on January 5, 1910. *Les Canadiens* got off to a fast start, defeating Cobalt 7–6 in overtime in the opening game. Alas, it was one of only two games they would win all season.

During their first season, the *Club de Hockey Canadien* wore blue jerseys with a narrow white band at the shoulder and chest and a large white "C" in front. Their pants were white and their stockings red.

The CHA, meanwhile, floundered from the beginning and most games attracted only a few hundred fans. After a mere two weeks of league play, in mid-January, team owners swallowed their pride and pleaded with the NHA clubs for admittance, suggesting total amalgamation as their salvation. But Ambrose O'Brien and James Gardner remembered how they were slighted by the rival-league operators a mere two months earlier. The NHA operators huddled and then agreed to admit only two franchises to their fold: Ottawa and the Montreal Shamrocks. When these clubs abandoned the CHA, the league folded.

O'Brien generously offered the defunct Nationals the opportunity of taking over *Les Canadiens* and was amazed when the answer was no. It ranks as one of the greatest missed opportunities in the history of sport.

A Montreal team emerged from that initial season covered with glory—but it wasn't *Les Canadiens*. Jimmy Gardner's Wanderers captured the league title (11 wins, one defeat) and went on to win the Stanley Cup. They also skated off with a glistening new trophy—the O'Brien Cup—made of silver from the O'Brien mines in Cobalt and valued at $6,000, far more than the $50 bowl Lord Stanley had donated to hockey before the turn of the century.

In 1910, when Montrealer George Kennedy and his partners in the Canadien Athletic Club purchased the Canadiens, the team emblem became a maple leaf with the letters "CAC" imprinted on the leaf. Imagine a maple leaf on a Montreal jersey! The sweater colours became red, white, and blue. By 1915 the sweater began to take on the appearance of the modern-day red sweater. In 1917 someone designed a large "C" surrounding a small "H"—an emblem which has remained constant, and extremely popular, for almost 80 years. There is a misconception that the letter "H" stands for "Habs" or

"Habitants," meaning farmers or people living in the country, stemming from the fact that most Canadiens were French-speaking boys from rural areas. But the "H" in the emblem really stands for "Hockey."

The Montreal Cup Game That Was Never Finished

Long before the Canadiens zoomed to hockey prominence, a Montreal team known as the Victorias held the Stanley Cup and turned back five different challengers who tried to wrest it from them. In 1899, the Winnipeg Vics journeyed east to battle the Montrealers in a two-game, total-goals series. The second game had a bizarre ending that left fans and officials totally perplexed and somewhat astonished.

In the opening match, the hometown Victorias squeezed out a 2–1 victory over the Winnipeggers, and in the second encounter, with only a few minutes to play, Montreal held a 3–2 lead. Winnipeg's star forward Tony Gingras rushed up the ice and hurled himself at the Montreal defence. Somehow he knifed through and the tying goal appeared to be his, when suddenly he crumpled to the ice, howling in pain. A burly Montreal defender, Bob McDougall, hot in pursuit and swinging his stick like a lumberjack, had clubbed Gingras across both legs.

The whistle blew. "Two minutes, Mr. McDougall," ruled referee Jim Findlay, a Montrealer.

"But I hardly touched him," protested McDougall.

"What!" screamed the Winnipeggers. "McDougall should get life imprisonment for such a dastardly blow. At least throw the dirty s.o.b. out of the game."

"Two minutes it is," answered the referee.

The furious Winnipeg players decided to leave the ice in protest. They retreated to their dressing room, where they hurled their sticks and gloves on the floor.

Findlay shrugged, then told the Stanley Cup officials he'd had enough of the players' shenanigans. So he took off his skates, hailed a horse-drawn sleigh outside the arena, and ordered the driver to take him home.

Bob McDougall made his way to the Winnipeg room, where he apologized profusely for injuring Gingras. Even though he'd come close to breaking both legs of the Winnipeg player, McDougall pleaded for forgiveness, saying he really hadn't meant to hurt the Winnipeg star. "Come on boys," he urged them. "Let's forgive and forget. We've got a game to finish. The Stanley Cup is at stake."

The visitors told McDougall to get lost. One or two wanted to beat him to a pulp and heave him bodily from their dressing room.

Meanwhile, in an effort to salvage the series, several officials leaped into sleighs and pursued Findlay to his home. There they pleaded with him to return and arbitrate the final few minutes of playing time. Finally the stubborn referee agreed to return. When he arrived back at the arena, he was surprised to find thousands of fans still huddled in their seats. "It's amazing," he told a friend. "After all, I've been gone for more than an hour and it's freezing in here. The outside temperature must be 20 below."

The referee pulled on his skates and pulled out his stopwatch. He gave the Winnipeg Vics 15 minutes to return to the ice. They said they'd do so on one condition. Findlay must banish McDougall from further play. Findlay said he wouldn't consider it and another heated discussion followed until Findlay looked at his watch.

"Time's up, gentlemen," he declared. "There'll be no more arguments and no more hockey. Winnipeg has forfeited the game. I've decided that Montreal shall retain the Cup. They are the winners and still champions."

For the second time on that evening of February 18, 1899, referee Jim Findlay pulled on his heavy coat, hoisted his skates over his shoulder, and walked off into the night.

First-Season Woes

The scoring sensation for *Les Canadiens* in their initial season (1909–10) was Edouard "Newsy" Lalonde, a native of Cornwall. He dazzled the fans with his brilliant rushes and collected goals with ease. Then, suddenly, he was gone. In mid-February, Renfrew made a deal with the Montreal club (Why not? Renfrew was financing both teams) and Lalonde joined Renfrew for the rest of the season. He led all NHA scorers with 38 goals in 11 games.

In their initial season, there was no indication the Canadiens would someday rule as hockey's premier power. The club finished last in the standings with a 2–10 record. The Canadiens' two goaltenders, Joe Cattarinich and Ted Groulx, turned in woeful goals-against averages of 7.7 and 8.6 respectively. Montreal's worst defeats were to Haileybury (15–3), Cobalt (11–7), and Wanderers (11–6). In the 15–3 defeat to Haileybury, Alex Currie and Nick Bawlf combined for 11 goals between them—Currie with six and Bawlf with five. In 12 games the team's beleaguered goaltenders allowed 100 goals. The only good news for Canadiens fans came after the season. The Renfrew team allowed Newsy Lalonde to return to Montreal—for a fee of $500.

What a bargain! Lalonde blazed his way through pro hockey, receiving more praise and condemnation than any other star. He had a nasty temper and tangled with all the hard-nosed players of his era. He once scored nine goals in a game, eight goals in a game, six goals in a game (three times), and five goals in a game (six times). He was the original Flying Frenchman and scored 416 career goals in 314 games. He was the Canadiens' captain when they won the Stanley Cup over Portland in 1916 and he was playing manager of the team in 1918 and 1919 when they won back-to-back NHL championships.

In 1922, following a disagreement with Leo Dandurand, one of the new owners of the Canadiens, Lalonde was traded to Saskatoon of the Western Canada Hockey League for Aurel Joliat, an amateur player under option to Saskatoon.

Montrealers Disfigure Stanley Cup

In a four-season span from 1906 through 1910, the Montreal Wanderers were the highest scoring machine in hockey. In league play during that stretch, they won 59 games and lost only nine. In the 1907 season, the Wanderers went undefeated in ten games and averaged over ten goals a game, scoring 105 times. No other team has ever come close to that mark. They won four Stanley Cup challenges in that span and might have won more. But in the spring of 1909, the Cup trustees ordered the Wanderers to hand the Cup over to Ottawa, champions of the Eastern Canada Hockey League, even though Ottawa had played no Cup matches that season. The Wanderers showed their displeasure in an unusual way. When the Cup was shipped to Ottawa for presentation to the new champions—the Senators—it bore some startling changes.

"Oh, look at this," said the Senators, when they examined the silverware. "Those damn Montreal Wanderers have scratched their names all over the trophy."

It was true. The Wanderers, using a special instrument, had carved their names inside the bowl in extra-large letters.

"The sons of bitches even added a few names on the Cup from their team of three seasons ago," said a furious Ottawa official. "There are small plates on the Cup for the engraving of the winning team and the year it was captured. The plates were deliberately ignored."

Another Ottawa official wailed, "Nobody gave the Wanderers permission to scratch their names all over this great trophy. It's inexcusable. Now there's no room left for the names of future winners."

While the Wanderers shrugged off accusations that they'd defaced the Cup, permission was sought and granted to have the bowl resilvered and returned to its original appearance.

The Goalie Wore No Gloves

Georges Vezina enjoyed a remarkable 15-year career in professional hockey. All of those years were spent with the Montreal Canadiens, who discovered the young netminder, a marvel of composure, while playing an exhibition game in Chicoutimi in the spring of 1910.

Vezina, already known as the Chicoutimi Cucumber because of his coolness under fire, stopped the famous Montrealers cold that night. Not a single puck entered his net. By the time the next season had rolled around, he'd signed a professional contract with the Canadiens, and he served as their net custodian for the next decade and a half, never missing a game.

One oddity about Vezina's career was that he didn't really learn how to skate until he was in his late teens. The idea of wearing skates held little appeal for him, especially when he could do the job in goal while wearing his sturdy work boots. Two years prior to his debut with the Canadiens, he was finally persuaded to conform and exchange his boots for blades during hockey games.

Vezina was married by the time he was 20 and in the tradition of French-Canadian families of his era, he began fathering babies like he was aiming at a world record. The Vezinas produced 22 little Vezinas before Mrs. Vezina said, "Georges, that's enough. Save some energy for the hockey games."

One of Vezina's sons was born on the very night the Canadiens won the Stanley Cup in 1916. Georges named the infant Stanley, of course, and within days had the little gaffer sitting in the bowl of the Stanley Cup posing for a photograph.

Vezina was a master at handling the hardest of shots and clearing the puck without giving up rebounds. He was hampered by a bizarre rule of the era that prohibited goalies from falling to the ice to block shots. It was only in the final three years of his career that the rule was erased from the book and he could flip and flop to his heart's content.

Several years ago I received a letter from a fan in Perth, Ontario, a man who witnessed Vezina play at the peak of his career on occasions when he faced the Ottawa Senators in Ottawa. The fan claims he saw Vezina play in several games—without gloves! It's a fascinating eyewitness observation but one that must be treated with some skepticism until further research confirms the claim. The fan wrote:

> Brian, my brother, and I used to go to all the games in Ottawa. Believe me, the rink there was no better than a barn. The wind would whistle through the cracks in the boards and I'm certain it would have been warmer standing out in the middle of the Rideau Canal. My brother and I would stand behind the wire netting in back of the goal when the Canadiens were playing Ottawa. My, how we loved to torment Vezina. I suppose it was because he was so good. We would bring our peashooters to the game and fire peas at Vezina's head whenever an Ottawa player had a chance to score.
>
> Vezina couldn't speak English but he sure knew how to curse in French, especially at us. Finally he got wise and pulled a small cap on his head. He would pull the cap around with the peak at the back to stop our peas from hitting him in the neck. It robbed us of a lovely target.
>
> In those days the goal judge stood on a small board placed behind the goalie's net. He was right out on the ice and many a time a player skating behind the net would send him flying—not always accidentally. And the peas we'd shoot would often hit the goal judge instead of Vezina.
>
> Believe it or not, Vezina wore no gloves. People today scoff when I tell them that. But he had a great pair of hands. The players today are sissies compared to the oldtimers. In my era it wasn't only the goalies who played a full sixty minutes and often overtime as well. All the players on the ice did. Those were the good old days.
>
> Best wishes,
>
> J. Tudor, Perth, Ontario

Wacky Events from the Past

On November 6, 1917, a few days before the NHL was formed, a man named E. W. Sheppard, president of the Arena in Montreal, stated that he was sick and tired of the "eternal bickering and squabbling" among member clubs of the NHA. Sheppard said, "Unless the two Montreal teams—the Canadiens and the Wanderers—can both produce teams of decent calibre, I shall bar professional hockey from my rink and reserve the ice time for skating purposes only."

During the 1905 season, the Montreal Wanderers signed a forward named Charlie Liffiton. Liffiton was thought to be so valuable that his team once arranged a special train to transport him to Ottawa for an important game. Liffiton left his day job at quitting time, raced to the station and sat alone in a special car that whisked him to Ottawa. When he reported to work the following Monday morning, his employer fired him, possibly for sneaking away from his desk a few minutes early.

When the Montreal Wanderers accepted a challenge from the Edmonton team in December, 1908—at the beginning of a new season—the Wanderers didn't know they'd be facing a team of "ringers." Edmonton showed up with a lineup of stars recruited from other teams; only one player, Fred Whitcroft at rover, had played on the Edmonton team during the regular season. The ringers included Bert Lindsay, Lester Patrick, Didier Pitre, Tom Phillips, and Harold McNamara, all future Hall-of-Famers. Even so, the Wanderers won the two-game, total goals to count series 13–10.

In 1908, the Montreal Wanderers were unwilling participants in a Stanley Cup series against an Ottawa team, the Vics. Wanderers management sneered at the poor calibre of the Vics and tried to avoid the match-up. A Montreal spokesman stated the games would have to begin at 10:30 p.m. because "the ice was not available any earlier." It was also suggested that the games be played behind closed doors. This infuriated the Cup trustees and the Vics. The Wanderers were ordered to play the series "in the normal manner and at a fitting time." They did and trounced the Vics 9–3 and 13–1. Ernie Russell of the Wanderers scored four goals in the first game and six in the second.

Bad Joe Hall, who died of the flu epidemic that forced cancellation of the Stanley Cup final series between the Canadiens and Seattle in 1919, was once a member of another Montreal club—the Shamrocks. In 1910, playing against Renfrew, Hall was banished from the game for attacking judge-of-play Rod Kennedy. Hall said he'd been cut over both eyes in a fight with Frank Patrick and, blinded by the blood, struck Kennedy thinking he was Patrick. The league refused to accept his excuse and fined him $100. Hall simply refused to pay the fine. A month later the league persuaded the Shamrocks to cover the debt—plus a sum of $27 to pay for a new suit for Kennedy. His had been torn in the fracas.

Prior to its second season of operation, the NHA established a salary cap of $5,000 per club. With ten players per team, this meant that the average salary of the NHA's players was $500. The new cap was a tremendous shock to the players, many of whom had earned over $1,000 the previous year. Art Ross noted that his salary over the past four seasons had jumped from $1,000 to $2,700. There was talk that the players would organize a strike and form a players' association and possibly even a new league (Art Ross wanted the Montreal franchise), but these threats were not taken seriously by the owners. One by one, the players caved in and signed with their old clubs.

In 1911, the manager of the Canadiens launched a law suit against the Canadian Pacific Railroad for $1,000. He accused the railroad of negligence in not getting the team equipment to Renfrew in time for an important game there.

For the 1912 season, the position of rover was eliminated, an idea suggested by a Montrealer, W. E. Northey. It may also have been Northey who suggested that players wear distinct numerals on their jerseys, although the Patrick brothers have been credited with the proposal. Hockey became the first of the team sports to adopt this idea. Initially, the numerals were attached to small armbands with a blackboard at rinkside listing the players' names and numbers for identification purposes. Small printed programs soon followed.

Prior to the 1912 season, it was agreed that the Canadiens would sign French-speaking players only. Other league clubs agreed to abstain from signing French players.

In 1914, Didier Pitre of the Canadiens threatened to sue the Montreal Star for libel after a sports reporter wrote some uncomplimentary things about the player and his lifestyle. The Canadiens promptly dealt Pitre to Vancouver as part of a deal that brought Newsy Lalonde back to Montreal after a one-season stint with Vancouver of the PCHL.

In February 1914, Leo Dandurand refereed a game between the Canadiens and Wanderers. Even though the Canadiens won the game 6–5 in overtime, manager George Kennedy of the Canadiens was irate over Dandurand's performance. Following the game, he rushed across the ice and assaulted the diminutive referee. Dandurand said, "He caught me with his fists before the fans and the players. Then he came back and insulted me in the worst manner in the umpire's room, calling me vile names before several witnesses."

A few months later, it was decided to lock the game officials in their dressing room between periods, to prevent managers, players, and fans from gaining access to them.

When the Canadiens met Seattle for the Stanley Cup in 1917, Newsy Lalonde was the villain in game two, won by Seattle 6–1. He was penalized five times and finally, in exasperation, skated up to the referee and slammed the butt of his stick into the ref's stomach. Lalonde was given a match penalty and fined $25, and was fortunate to escape a long suspension. Seattle won the series three games to one.

When the NHA disbanded in 1917 and was replaced by the NHL, franchises were granted to the Canadiens, the Wanderers, Ottawa, and a new team in Toronto. Quebec opted out and the Quebec players were dispersed throughout the league, with the Wanderers having first choice because of their lowly position in the previous season's standings. Incredibly, the Wanderers passed on Joe Malone, who a few weeks earlier had scored eight goals against them in a single game and had finished as top scorer in the NHA with 41 goals in 19 games. Malone was snapped up by the Canadiens and promptly set a remarkable NHL record with 44 goals in 20 games.

Chapter 2
THE TURBULENT TWENTIES

Illness Ends Series in Seattle

In the spring of 1919, for the first time in its long history, the Stanley Cup was without a home. The famous trophy had been shipped to Seattle, Washington, where it was to be awarded to the winners of the Seattle-Montreal series. The series turned into one of the most bizarre match-ups in the history of hockey. It was a hard-fought, hard-luck series—and it had a tragic ending.

The Canadiens and the Seattle Metropolitans were evenly matched. After five games, each team had won two games and another had ended in a tie. Montreal's Newsy Lalonde was the scoring star in game two, potting all four Habs goals. The fourth game ended in a rare scoreless tie despite an hour and forty minutes of overtime. Some reporters called it the greatest game ever played on the Pacific Coast. In that game a few of the players appeared to be labouring, and with good reason. The dreaded Spanish flu epidemic, which swept across North America that year, had struck the Stanley Cup playoffs. Several players—more Canadiens than Metropolitans—were so afflicted that they could barely skate.

In game five the Canadiens eked out a 4–3 victory to knot the finals at two wins apiece. By now the demanding series had produced more flu victims as well as a number of serious injuries. In mid-game, Montreal's "Bad Joe" Hall staggered off the ice and was rushed to a nearby hospital. He was followed by teammate Jack McDonald. After the game, five of the Canadiens required medical attention and Manager George Kennedy also complained of feeling poorly.

But Kennedy desperately wanted the Stanley Cup. When league officials decided to suspend the series and call it a tie, Kennedy protested. "Let me borrow some lads from the Victoria club," he pleaded. "I'll put them in Montreal uniforms and we'll finish this thing yet." But the Seattle executives vetoed his proposal and instructed workers to begin removing the ice from the arena.

In a display of sportsmanship, the Seattle club officials declined to claim Lord Stanley's trophy. Technically, they could have commandeered it on the grounds that Montreal did not have enough players available for the deciding game. After much discussion, the Stanley Cup trustees decided that Toronto, winners of the Cup in 1918, would be allowed to retain the trophy for another year.

With their season over, a solemn band of Canadiens, some bruised and battered, others pale and haggard from the effects of the flu, boarded their train for the long return journey to Montreal. Left behind in hospital was 38-year-old Joe Hall, whose condition was described as serious. A few hours after the departure of his mates, Hall suffered a fateful setback. He was found to be suffering from pneumonia, and within days he was dead.

"Bad Joe" Hall was never as bad as his nickname might suggest. Born in England, he played hockey in Canada and the United States at the top level for more than 15 years, having begun with Winnipeg and Brandon teams. He was a tenacious checker—hence the nickname. Frank Patrick, president of the Pacific Coast Hockey League, said of Hall, "The game of hockey suffered a huge loss with his passing. Off the ice he was one of the jolliest, best-hearted, most popular men who ever played the game."

Hall left a wife and three children.

A Shy Little Guy Almost Gives Up

In Stratford and Mitchell, Ontario, where he grew up, Howie Morenz was known as a shy little fellow who almost gave up the game he loved before he ever got started.

Morenz and his family had moved from Mitchell to Stratford when Howie was in high school. When asked to try out for a local Stratford team, Morenz showed up with only skates and a stick, for he had no other equipment—not even gloves. In the scrimmage that followed he was belted around by the heavier, well-padded players on the ice and he left the tryout in tears. He showed his bruised and bleeding hands to the coach and told him he was not coming back. Then he threw his skates over his shoulder and walked out into the night.

He stayed away from hockey for some time, until the Stratford boys ran into some old rivals from Kitchener and suffered a bad beating. The coach realized he needed an offensive star and recalled that young Morenz had shown some promise in the brief tryout he'd been given. He called Morenz and promised to find him some hand-me-down equipment if he'd give hockey another try. Morenz agreed to come back. In the return match with Kitchener, he was the outstanding player on the ice.

Soon he was playing amateur hockey with three teams in Stratford and his potential was such that Ernest Sauve, a referee, tipped off the Montreal Canadiens. "You better grab this kid," said Sauve. "He's a great-looking prospect."

Young Morenz had no burning desire to play professional hockey. He enjoyed small-town life in Stratford. It took a visit from Cecil Hart, who would later become coach of the Canadiens, to convince young Morenz to commit his hockey future to Montreal. The fact that Hart dropped $850 in Morenz's lap helped to settle the matter.

He became an instant fan favourite in Montreal—the fastest man on ice. His highest-scoring season was 1929–30 when he collected 40 goals. On three occasions he captured the Hart Trophy as the NHL's most valuable player. Twice he led the league in scoring, and he played on three Stanley Cup–winning teams.

Montreal fans never forgave management for trading Morenz to Chicago in 1934. After he spent a season as a Blackhawk and another season split between Chicago and New York, the Canadiens heeded the wishes of their fans and reacquired Morenz for what turned out to be his final campaign.

Habs Win Game in Record Time

Hockey has always been a 60-minute game. But one night in 1921, the Canadiens won an NHL contest in record time: 55 minutes.

On January 26, 1921, the out-manned Ottawa Senators were clinging to a lead over the Canadiens in the third period of a game in Montreal. But the Ottawa boys were tiring because they had only one substitute player on their bench, a kid named McKell. The Habs had four subs on their roster.

There was ill feeling right from the start. The Senators were seething because of a pregame ruling by Habs owner George Kennedy that barred Punch Broadbent from bolstering the Ottawa lineup. Why Kennedy had the right to ban Broadbent from the contest isn't made clear in the newspaper accounts of the match, but he did. And a good thing too, for Broadbent was a scorer. The following season he would score 25 goals in 16 consecutive games, an NHL record that remains safe in the books to this day, despite the exploits of Wayne Gretzky and Mario Lemieux.

Without Broadbent, the Senators frustrated the Montrealers with their patented "kitty bar the door" strategy.

Late in the game, a Montreal player pushed the puck past Ottawa goalie Clint Benedict to tie the score 3–3. Ottawa players screamed that the goalie was illegally scored on but referee Cooper Smeaton turned a deaf ear.

He faced the puck at centre ice and play resumed . . . at least by one of the teams. The Ottawa men, still furious at Smeaton, made no effort to go after the puck. They stood idly by while Montreal scored the go-ahead goal. Still sulking, they watched Montreal add an insurance marker. By then, the Senators had had enough.

They told Smeaton they would not play another second unless he stepped aside and let another official take over. "You can do what you want," replied Smeaton, "but you'll be dealing with me until this game is over."

With that, the Ottawa players left the ice for their dressing room and Smeaton promptly awarded the game to Montreal. The final score was 5–3.

But the fans were so enraged by the actions of the Ottawa players that they almost rioted. While some chased after the Ottawa players, threatening to pummel them, others turned venomous toward the Ottawa fans in the crowd. The latter, frightened by the ugly mood of the mob, scurried like rabbits for the exits.

When the game was halted, there were still five minutes and 13 seconds to be played.

The Goat of the Game—Temporarily

Newsy Lalonde, one of the greatest of the old Canadiens, made one of the most glaring mistakes in NHL history one night in 1920. He was the goat of the game—but not for long. Overtime would bring forgiveness.

Newsy once confessed he deliberately scored a goal against his own team. In retirement, he recalled the embarrassing moment this way. "Lots of players have deflected or kicked a puck into their own team's net and it's always accidental. But I deliberately shot the tying goal past Georges Vezina, my own goaltender, one night in Montreal."

Could it be true? How could a player do such a thing? A search through the NHL records brought me back to January 29, 1920, and a game between Montreal and Quebec. Canadiens were leading 3–2 with a couple of minutes left to play in the third period. Joe Malone, the Quebec scoring ace, sifted through and blazed a shot at Vezina, who made a miraculous save. The puck rebounded off the goalie's stick and landed at the feet of Lalonde, who stood directly in front of the Montreal net.

"I thought I heard the whistle blow when I snapped up the loose puck," Lalonde said later. "So I relaxed. Then I playfully moved in on Vezina, deked him aside and slipped the puck past him into the net. What a gaffe! There'd been no whistle. I turned around and all the players were staring at me as if I was demented. The astonished goal judge waved his hand in the air, signalling the tying goal and Harvey Pulford, the equally surprised referee, confirmed the decision. Imagine my anguish and the flow of language I used as I chased the referee all the way to centre ice, trying to explain myself. But Pulford would not be swayed. He was adamant. The goal would count. It was my most embarrassing moment in hockey."

Reading on, I discovered that Lalonde hadn't completed the story he'd begun. It turned out the goat's horns were a temporary part of his hockey attire. In the overtime, he discarded them to become the hero of the night. He made an end-to-end rush, squirmed his way through the Quebec defence, enticed goalie Brophy out of his net, and whacked the puck past him for the winning goal.

"The friendly pounding I received from my teammates after the winning goal was nice," recalled Lalonde. "Much nicer than the pounding I might have received if I hadn't scored it."

The Habs Are Sold for $11,000

One of the stories Leo Dandurand liked to tell was how he and two partners purchased the Montreal Canadiens—without knowing it.

Following the death of owner George Kennedy (also known as George Kendall) in 1921, the Canadiens franchise was put up for sale. There were three bidders for the club. In addition to the trio of Messrs. Dandurand, Cattarinich, and Letourneau, Tom Duggan came forward representing the Mount Royal Arena and Frank Calder, NHL president, spoke for a group from Ottawa.

Calder pleaded with Kennedy's widow not to sell the franchise until he could contact his principals in Ottawa. It seems they were on a hunting trip, miles away from a telephone. Calder apparently had been authorized to bid $8,500 on their behalf.

Dandurand and his partners were also out of town, doing racetrack business in Cleveland. Their representative at the auction was Cecil Hart, a prominent Montreal businessman. He'd been authorized to bid $10,000 for the club.

Tom Duggan impressed the widow Kennedy by placing ten crisp new bills on the table, each of $1,000 denomination. "It's a huge sum of money to pay for a hockey team," he said, "but I'm prepared to do it."

Cecil Hart spoke up before Mrs. Kennedy could stash the bills in her purse. "Let me call Mr. Dandurand in Cleveland and see if he'll agree to increase Mr. Duggan's offer," he suggested. Hart suspected the Dandurand group was about to lose out on the investment of a lifetime.

When Hart called, Dandurand told him to keep on bidding but to use his own good judgement, reminding him that $11,000 was a lot to pay for a hockey team.

Hart returned to the meeting room and told Mrs. Kennedy and her representative that the Dandurand group would offer $11,000 and not a penny more.

When Mrs. Kennedy turned to Duggan, he shook his head. "No, no, it's too much," he said, sweeping his bills off the table. "I'm not going to get involved in a bidding war with the Dandurand group." And he stormed from the room.

Did the Dandurand group celebrate their triumph? Not at all. For some reason, Cecil Hart didn't contact them until the following day. Only then did they learn that they owned an NHL hockey team—the most famous one of all. And it wasn't until the end of the following season, when the team showed a profit of $18,000, that they realized what a wonderful bargain they'd made.

Many years later the club was sold to the Canadian Arena Company for $165,000. That too proved to be a real bargain.

Joliat Lucky to Leave Town Alive

One of Montreal's greatest early-day stars was little Aurel Joliat. The Mighty Atom, a native of Ottawa, came east from Saskatoon to join the Habs in the spring of 1923, replacing Newsy Lalonde, who had been sold to the western club.

For the next 16 seasons, Joliat toiled for the Habs, often lining up with Howie Morenz to provide Forum fans with some of the most astonishing playmaking and scoring ever seen.

Montrealers never knew how fortunate they were to have a hale and hearty Joliat in their midst. For he never told them of that night in Iroquois Falls, and how he escaped the wrath of two seedy gents bent on murdering him.

Here's what happened. Joliat, fresh from a good season in amateur hockey, went west from Ottawa to seek his fortune. His path took him to Iroquois Falls, where he hooked up with an intermediate team. The Falls team was scheduled to play a championship match against a rival club and

Joliat was approached on the afternoon of the match.

Two sinister-looking types whispered an offer in his ear. They'd give little Aurel $500 if he'd throw the game and let the rival team win.

Joliat asked for a peek at the cash because he'd never seen $500 before. The wad was flashed and Joliat couldn't help himself; he grabbed the money and pocketed it.

The gamblers showed up at rinkside, satisfied that the many bets they'd made would pay off handsomely. Joliat showed up with a train ticket in his pocket and his travelling bag packed.

Iroquois Falls won the game easily, thanks to Joliat's six-goal scoring spree. After the match, the gamblers fought their way through the jubilant crowd to the Falls' dressing room. It was clear they had murder on their minds. But their intended victim proved to be just as slippery a target in street shoes as he was on skates.

While the gamblers seethed outside the dressing-room door, Joliat slipped out another exit, raced to the railroad station, and climbed aboard the night train headed west. Only when he reached Regina did his pulse return to normal. Needless to say, he never went back to Iroquois Falls.

Putting one over on a pair of gamblers may have been Joliat's inspiration for some of his on-ice shenanigans. Throughout his long career he was noted for taunting opponents, needling them until they ended up making mistakes and wearing goat horns. As one wag put it, "Joliat was so good at getting guys to mess up he should have started a goat farm."

When Aurel Joliat hung up his skates at the close of the 1937–38 NHL season, hockey lost one of its most picturesque characters. Joliat's career as a left winger extended over 16 years of play at the major-league level, and he was always a superstar. Joliat was often the target of opponents, for he wore a little black cap on his head—a cap with a peak—like a baseball player. Opposing players, when Joliat sifted by, would swipe at that cap with a gloved hand, and if they dislodged it, a mighty roar of yeahs and boos was bound to follow. Infuriated by this lack of respect, Joliat would retrieve his cap, cover his bald spot with it, and vow to make the hated rival suffer. Sometimes he did it by scoring one of his patented goals; more often he cracked the cap-disturber across the ankles with a two-hander—hard enough to make him think twice about a repeat offence.

They called Joliat the Mighty Atom of hockey and it was no misnomer. He weighed in at 130 pounds. He was a marvellous stickhandler and had an unusual abundance of "hockey sense," which is simply a way of saying that he did the right thing at the right time.

One Montreal writer of his era said, "He rolled away from 200-pounders, faded from the path of charging rivals and sidestepped and hurdled his way clear of smashing body-blows, flying elbows and jabbing butt-ends. His amazing quickness saved him from untold punishment over the years and kept him going, like a brook, apparently forever."

Was Cleghorn the Toughest of Them All?

Mention the name Sprague Cleghorn to oldtimers—I mean *real* oldtimers, because there are precious few left who saw him play—and they'll tell you he was the meanest son of a bitch who ever played the game.

I first heard about Cleghorn in the '60s, when I was working on King Clancy's autobiography. Clancy infuriated the Montreal star one night in Ottawa with a cute little trick. The impish teenage rookie was chasing after Cleghorn, who had only one Ottawa defenceman to beat. When he charged into the defender, Clancy whistled for a pass. Without breaking stride, Cleghorn passed the puck to Clancy. King whirled around and led a rush in the opposite direction while the crowd roared with laughter at the deception and jeered Cleghorn's gaffe.

Clancy told me, "Cleghorn glared at me at the time but the incident was soon forgotten, at least by me. When the period ended, and I was leaving the ice, I heard a voice behind me. 'Oh, King, you forgot something.' I turned to see what I'd forgot and wham! Every light in the rink went out. Cleghorn hit me so hard I woke up to see a priest standing over me. I thought he was giving me the last rites. I heard later my teammates tried to get at Sprague and he told them, 'Honest, guys, I just went over to pat King on the head— to let him know he was playing a swell game.'" If that was so, it's the first pat on the head that required a bucket of water to revive a guy and brought a priest out of the stands.

Jack Adams, Detroit's manager, bristled at the mention of Cleghorn's name. "The bastard was an unwashed surgeon," he once told writer Trent Frayne. "If you were lucky enough to skate by him he'd turn and hook his stick across your face or crack you over the head."

Red Dutton, who once served as league president, played against Cleghorn in the Stanley Cup finals of 1924. "If some of the goons I see with long hair in modern day hockey ever met Cleghorn," Dutton told Frayne, "He'd shave them to the skull. Jesus, he was mean. You never wanted to fall in front of Sprague because he'd kick your balls off."

Charles Coleman, author of *The Trail of the Stanley Cup*, writes about a game that Sprague Cleghorn and his brother Odie played in Ottawa one night in 1921: "In this game Cleghorn made a shambles of the Ottawa team with some assistance from his brother. A vicious swing at Eddie Gerard cut him over the eye for five stitches. Nighbor was charged and in falling damaged his elbow. A butt end for Cy Denneny required several stitches over his eye and more in his nose. This worked out to a match foul and a $15 fine for Sprague. The Ottawa police offered to arrest Sprague and charge him with assault. Lou Marsh, the referee, said he could handle the situation without police interference. Later he wrote in his report that he considered the Cleghorn brothers to be a disgrace to the game of hockey."

A season later, in a playoff game versus Ottawa, Cleghorn and Lionel Hitchman tried to carve divots in each other's head with their sticks. With time running out, Cleghorn wanted a final crack at Hitchman. He charged the Ottawa player and smashed him in the face with a cross check that left Hitchman on the ice unconscious, blood flowing from his wounds. Without waiting for the NHL to punish Cleghorn, Leo Dandurand stepped in and suspended him. At the same time he suspended Bill Coutu, another Canadien with a nasty disposition. Both men missed the follow-up game with Ottawa, despite pleading with Dandurand to relent and let them perform.

Cleghorn apparently brought his anger home with him. In 1918, while recuperating from a broken leg, he was arrested after his wife filed a charge against him claiming he whacked her with his crutch. A few days later, the charge was dismissed.

Dandurand Suspends Own Players After Brutal Playoff Game

On March 7, 1923, the Montreal Canadiens hosted the Ottawa Senators in the first game of a two-game playoff series with total goals to count. That opening match ranks as one of the most violent in Montreal hockey history. Immediately following the bloody affair, Habs owner Leo Dandurand suspended and fined two of his star players, Sprague Cleghorn and Billy Coutu (sometimes called Couture), for the excessive brutality they'd perpetrated against the visitors.

All attendance records for a game in Montreal (to that time) were smashed when over 7,000 packed the Mount Royal Arena for the series opener. Hundreds of fans had to be turned away. After the match, angry spectators invaded the ice surface and dozens of fights broke out between Montreal and Ottawa supporters. Even the playing of the national anthem failed to stop the brawling. Finally, reserve policemen rushed in and attempted to restore peace.

A Montreal alderman in attendance stated later, "The affair is a blot on the face of genuine sport in Montreal. The police should have halted play and made arrests long before the game concluded."

From the outset it was apparent that the Canadiens were in a foul mood and intent on giving the invaders from Ottawa a rough ride. Billy Coutu was the most violent offender. He drew a match penalty for deliberately smashing Ottawa's Denneny over the head with his stick after the latter scored the first goal of the game. Coutu's explosive temper would, incidentally, later cost him his NHL career. In 1927, playing for Boston, he smashed a referee in the face and was suspended for life.

Referee Lou Marsh, who handed out 12 penalties to Montreal and only two to Ottawa, was roasted by the Montreal fans and spent most of his time on the ice dodging bottles and other missiles thrown at him. Twice the game was stopped for the ice to be cleared of debris.

When Darragh scored a goal for Ottawa in the third period, Cleghorn exploded in anger. He carved Hitchman over the head with his stick and the Ottawa player had to be carried from the ice, bleeding profusely from a scalp wound. In the dressing room, Hitchman fainted and was taken to hospital under a police escort. There he was found to be suffering from a severe concussion.

Referee Marsh was fortunate to escape with his life. When he stepped from the ice at the end of the game, a wild-eyed spectator who'd been verbally abusing him all evening blocked his way and then punched him in the mouth. The irate fan, and thousands like him, wanted to pummel Marsh because he'd forced the Canadiens to play shorthanded for 41 of the 60 minutes. At one point, only three Canadiens were on the ice battling six Ottawa opponents.

Dandurand told reporters that Marsh was the cause of all the trouble and if Marsh was assigned to handle the return game in Ottawa the Canadiens would not show up. President Calder confidently predicted, "Dandurand and the Canadiens will show up all right. Really, the joke's on them because it was Montreal who moved that Marsh be appointed to this series in the first place."

The Habs' Odie Cleghorn told reporters he was furious with Dandurand for suspending his brother Sprague. He threatened a mutiny by stating, "Either Dandurand retracts everything he said about us, especially my brother, or you can bet that none of us will go to Ottawa. He is trying to make goats out of us and we will not stand for that. And that is absolutely final."

But it was far from final. Dandurand retracted nothing, and the players, including Odie Cleghorn, fell into line and meekly boarded the train for the return match in Ottawa.

Prior to the second game Sprague Cleghorn and Billy Coutu pleaded with Dandurand to let them play, but the owner was adamant. The fines and suspensions would stick.

The Canadiens, playing fast, clean hockey, edged Ottawa 2–1 in the return match, but Ottawa captured the NHL championship series three goals to two.

Forum Built for Maroons but Habs Play There First

When the construction of the original Montreal Forum neared completion in the fall of 1924, the Montreal Canadiens were not its first tenants, the Montreal Maroons were. The Maroons, owned by the Canadian Arena Company, had been granted a franchise in the league through the generosity of Leo Dandurand, who had a grand vision of a unique hockey rivalry between the Maroons and his Canadiens, one that would last for decades.

The Habs, locked into a contract to use the Mount Royal Arena, watched enviously as the huge edifice took shape. The original Forum, designed by architect John S. Archibald, cost $1.5 million, contained an artificial ice-making plant, and held seats for 9,300 fans.

The Habs' home opener was scheduled for November 29, 1924, against Toronto, but mild weather in Montreal turned the Mount Royal Arena into a swimming pool. Leo Dandurand acted swiftly and made arrangements to move the opening game to the new Forum, which guaranteed solid ice for the event. Despite heated protests from officials of the Mount Royal Arena, Dandurand moved players and equipment over to the Forum. As a result, it was the Habs and not the Maroons who played the inaugural game in the new ice palace. Over 8,000 fans witnessed the match, won by the Canadiens 7–1 over the Toronto St. Pats. The Forum was the first major-league arena designed expressly for hockey, and it would serve Montreal fans well for the next 72 seasons.

The Canadiens moved into the Forum permanently in 1926. Today's hockey fans have never seen anything like the rivalry that existed between the Canadiens and the Maroons. Heated? It was explosive. When the English-backed Maroons met the French-supported Canadiens, the on-ice battles were often overshadowed by skirmishes in the stands. Emotions became so feverish that a missed goal or an "undeserved" penalty would trigger a rash of pushes and punches, with police and ushers rushing in to keep English and French fans apart. The damage was usually minimal: a torn jacket, a hat yanked off and thrown away, the occasional black eye, and enough '20s-style "trash talk" (in two languages) to shock fans ten rows away.

It was the genius of Dandurand that created the rivalry—and the friction. He sanctioned a second NHL franchise for the city. It cost the Maroons' Jimmy Strachan a mere $15,000 for the privilege of sharing the Canadiens' territorial rights to Montreal. Dandurand once said, "I assumed that an English team competing against the mostly French Canadiens would turn into the biggest rivalry in the NHL—and it did."

The Maroons were the first of the two Forum tenants to taste Stanley Cup success. They captured the trophy in 1926 by defeating the Victoria Cougars in the finals on the Forum's artificial ice. It marked the last time a team representing another league was a Cup challenger. In 34 years, no less than 14 leagues had been represented in Cup playoffs.

The following year the Canadiens and the Maroons met in a memorable two-game playoff series, which the Canadiens won two goals to one after 12 minutes of overtime. Howie Morenz scored the winner, and each game attracted an estimated crowd of 11,000. The Habs were then eliminated by Ottawa, and the Senators went on to capture the Stanley Cup.

In 1928 the Canadiens finished first in the Canadian Division standings but were upset by the Maroons in the two-game playoff, three goals to two. Somehow, an estimated 13,000 fans packed the Forum for each encounter.

That was the season that the Maroons were edged three games to two in the finals against the Rangers. In game two, Rangers goalie Lorne Chabot was struck over the eye by a Nels Stewart shot. He was replaced by 44-year-old Lester Patrick, the New York coach. The Rangers won the game in overtime and went on to win the series and the Cup. By then the Maroons and the Canadiens were having financial problems, the Forum was mortgaged to its rafters, and there was talk of turning it into a streetcar barn.

When the Maroons withdrew from the NHL in 1938 (Leaf owner Conn Smythe vetoed a plan to move the team to St. Louis), the Canadiens had the Forum all to themselves. Over time they created hundreds of memorable moments within its walls. Twelve of Montreal's 24 Stanley Cup triumphs were celebrated on its ice surface, plus two more by the Maroons. The Maroons and the Red Wings started a playoff game at the Forum on March

24, 1936, and finished it in the early morning hours of March 25, in the sixth overtime period—the longest league or playoff game ever played.

On a March day the following year, the building became a cathedral when a multitude of fans, fighting back tears, filed solemnly past the bier of superstar Howie Morenz, whose sudden passing shocked millions. The building withstood a barrage of rocks and bottles hurled at it by rioting fans on the night of March 17, 1955, following the suspension of Rocket Richard and the termination of a game with Detroit.

There were league and team records established by Hab legends like Rocket Richard, Jacques Plante, Jean Beliveau, Steve Shutt, Guy Lafleur, and others. On New Year's Eve, 1975, a superb exhibition game between the Canadiens and the Soviet Red Army team (a 3–3 tie) prompted veteran observers to call it "one of the best hockey games ever played." The Habs outshot the touring Soviets 38–13 and controlled most of the play, but some fabulous saves by Vladislav Tretiak, who outshone Ken Dryden, kept the visitors from certain defeat.

By then the Forum looked nothing like the original arena. In 1946, when Frank Selke was lured to Montreal from Toronto, he dedicated himself to renovating the Forum. He ordered new plumbing installed ("The place stinks," he complained, "especially the rest rooms"). And the drab brown paint that seemed to be everywhere soon was covered over with much brighter colours.

In 1968 further renovations and additions costing $10 million brought the Forum's seating capacity up to 16,500. This became the arena we knew and loved until its doors closed on March 11, 1996. On that night a flaming torch was passed from hand to hand, to and from former captains Butch Bouchard, Maurice Richard, Jean Beliveau, Henri Richard, Yvan Cournoyer, Serge Savard, Bob Gainey, Guy Carbonneau, and, finally, incumbent Pierre Turgeon. The ovation for Maurice Richard was so prolonged that it left the Hall-of-Famer with tears in his eyes, his emotions in turmoil.

A few days later, and a mile closer to the heart of the city, the new Molson Centre opened. With seating for more than 21,000—5,000 more than the Forum—the $230-million facility is the largest arena in Canada. The new ice palace contains 135 luxury suites, 2,674 club seats, and three restaurants, and features a dramatic, eight-sided scoreboard over centre ice, with replays shown on four giant screens.

Vezina's Farewell Visit to the Forum

Georges Vezina's final NHL game was against the Pittsburgh Pirates on November 28, 1925. It was Montreal's first home game of the season and it would turn out to be Vezina's final appearance in a Montreal uniform, although no one knew it at the time. Vezina had played every league game (190) and playoff game (25) since joining the club and most fans assumed he would go on forever. But he was suffering from chest pains as he skated out to open the new season and collapsed to the ice during the first period. The game was delayed while trainers carried the ailing netminder to the medical room. Fans murmured their concern, for no Montreal player was more popular than the cool cage custodian from Chicoutimi.

Tests were taken and the news was not good. Vezina was told he was suffering from tuberculosis, a common and often fatal disease of his era. Team doctors, noting he'd played with a temperature of 102 in his final start and that he'd lost 35 pounds since training camp, ordered him to retire from hockey. His lungs, they said grimly, were in dreadful condition.

Told that his chances of survival were slim, the grim-faced goalie paid a final visit to the Canadiens' dressing room. He sat in his familiar corner and stared at his worn goal pads and skates, placed in their usual spot by trainer Eddie Dufour. Then the tears began to roll down his cheeks. Manager Leo Dandurand approached, placed a hand on his shoulder, and said, "Is there anything I can do for you, Georges?" Vezina wiped his eyes and said, "Yes, Leo, I would like to go home now. And I would like to take my Montreal sweater with me, the one I wore in the Stanley Cup finals in '24." The coveted jersey was quickly found and handed to him. Choking with emotion, he waved good-bye to his mates and left the room, never to return.

Dandurand made a brief statement to reporters. "Georges is gone and I doubt if hockey will ever know his like again. He has been a great credit to professional sport. He was a great athlete and a wonderful gentleman."

Vezina returned to his home in Chicoutimi, where he passed away four months later, on March 26, 1926. Later that year, Leo Dandurand, Louis Letourneau, and Joe Cattarinich donated the Vezina Trophy to the NHL in memory of the beloved goaltender.

Visitors to my hockey museum in Niagara Falls, Ontario, when they see the caption under Vezina's photo, often ask me the derivation of his unusual nickname—the Chicoutimi Cucumber. "That's easy," I explain. "He was born in Chicoutimi, Quebec, and in goal he was cool as a cucumber. Simple as that."

A Worthy Successor to Vezina

Perhaps it's poetic justice that Montreal goaltenders have won the Vezina Trophy more times than netminders from other NHL clubs. The coveted award is named after the Habs' first great netminder, the legendary Georges Vezina, who died in 1926. Were it not for the Vezina Trophy, the memory of one of the NHL's first great stars might have faded like the print in old press clippings.

The first winner of the Vezina Trophy was another George—George Hainsworth, Vezina's protege with the Canadiens. Hainsworth won it for three straight years, and no wonder: his goaltending stats are almost unbelievable. In his rookie season—1926–27—Hainsworth racked up 14 shutouts in

44 games and compiled a goals-against average of 1.52. He was even better in his sophomore season, with a 1.05 goals-against average and 13 shutouts. And in year three he was phenomenal, establishing a league record of 22 shutouts in 44 games and a minuscule goals-against average of 0.98. In the entire history of the NHL, no goalie but Hainsworth has ever held opposing shooters to less than one goal per game on average.

He almost lost his bid for his 22nd shutout in the second to last game of the season against the Maroons. With the Habs leading 1–0 and with less than a minute to play, the Maroons' Earl Robinson swept through the Canadiens' defence and blasted a shot at Hainsworth. Little George leaped in front of it and blocked it, but he failed to smother the rebound. Another Maroon, Dave Trottier, swept in and fired the puck toward an open corner of the net. Somehow, Hainsworth sprawled across his crease and tipped the puck to the far side of the goal post. That month, in six games, he was undefeated and gave up three goals.

What made Hainsworth's performances even more remarkable was the fact they came late in his hockey life. He was past 30 when Vezina collapsed and was forced to retire, giving way to the Ontario native. It took the Toronto-born Hainsworth, a pint-sized (5 feet 6 inches) refugee from Saskatoon of the WCHL, a long time to earn Vezina's sweater number 1. In his first three seasons, Hainsworth wore number 12, 14, 2, 12 again, and finally number 1. After 49 shutouts in 132 games, management decided he'd earned Vezina's old jersey number.

But every goalie has his bad nights, and Hainsworth encountered one in Boston in February 1933. He was riddled for ten goals by the Boston Bruins and later admitted "some of those goals were soft ones." Leo Dandurand, his boss, had seen enough. A few days later he traded Hainsworth to Toronto in return for lanky Lorne Chabot, another netminder.

By then Hainsworth was approaching 40. Still, he had three good seasons in Toronto even though he fell out of favour with team owner Conn Smythe. Smythe released him outright in 1937 and he returned to Montreal to play a few more games before retiring from hockey. Hainsworth was killed in a head-on car accident in 1950. He was 55.

A Rousing Start

In 1925–26, long before first-year NHL players vied for the Calder Trophy, a big, roughhousing centre named Nels Stewart made a memorable debut in the NHL. Until Gretzky, Lemieux, and Lindros came along, no other rookie established himself so quickly. Stewart amassed 34 goals in 36 games for the Montreal Maroons during an era when defence was paramount. Stewart not only won the NHL scoring title with 42 points, outscoring such luminaries as Aurel Joliat and Howie Morenz of the Canadiens (each with 26 points), but he was awarded the Hart Trophy as the league's MVP. Stewart switched to defence for the playoffs that year and led all scorers with six goals in eight games as the Maroons swept to the Stanley Cup over Victoria. If there'd been a Conn Smythe Trophy up for grabs in that era, the rookie would have won that one too.

Chapter 3
YEARS OF WOE

Aurel Joliat: 130 Pounds of Might and Muscle

"Oldtime hockey players like me were the dumbest bunch of athletes in the world," Aurel Joliat once said. "We never got paid what we deserved and most of us didn't have sense enough to save what money we got."

Joliat, then 85, was reminiscing about the pioneer days of the NHL and his career with the Canadiens. Born in Ottawa, he joined the Habs in 1922 (traded for a fading Newsy Lalonde) and played left wing on a line with Howie Morenz and Billy Boucher. He stayed around until 1938, when he retired as the highest-scoring left winger in history, with 270 goals.

"Retired hell!" he'd often snort. "They fired me when the Montreal Maroons folded and some of their players moved over to the Canadiens. I'm still damn mad about that."

"And don't say I played with Morenz," he added with a wink. "Although I tried to. Morenz was so fast I had to scoot well ahead of him on a rush or I was always lagging behind him, trying to catch up. Nobody ever played with Morenz." Was Aurel a tough hockey player? He proved that as a teenager when he fell off a roof, tumbled 35 feet to the ground, and landed on his back. He played 13 seasons in the NHL with two displaced vertebrae, which caused him great pain and forced him to wear an elaborate truss at all times. Then there were stomach ulcers that he mostly ignored. He was tough enough to become a star kicker with his hometown Ottawa Rough Riders, until a broken leg caused him to think seriously about concentrating full-time on hockey.

"Well, I guess I was tough enough," he once said. "You had to be to survive. But I wasn't the toughest. That mule-headed sonofabitch Eddie Shore was the meanest, toughest player I ever met. I was rushin' up the ice at the Forum one night when my lights went out. Shore hit me with a check that almost killed me. I was what? 130 pounds at the time and he musta been 190. He dislocated my shoulder and they carried me off in a lot of pain. Then I look around and Shore is leading a fancy rush. Forget the sore shoulder. I leaped over the boards and intercepted the big bugger. Hit him with a flyin' tackle. Hit him so hard he was out cold on the ice. He had it comin' I'd say..."

Joliat led the NHL in goals with 29 in 1925, played on three Stanley Cup teams, and was named MVP in 1934. Strangely, when the Habs won back-to-back Stanley Cups in 1930 and 1931, Joliat failed to score in any of the 16 games. In 1985, 60 years after he played in the opening game at the Montreal Forum, he was invited back as an honorary member of the Canadiens' "dream team." Then aged 83, he delighted the fans with a display of vigorous skating and stickhandling. He even took a couple of pratfalls, one of them caused by the red carpet laid on the ice. "The ghost of Eddie Shore must have put that damn rug in front of me," he would mutter.

The late Bill Galloway, a hockey historian and one of Joliat's best friends, recalled a time when Joliat, then in his 70s, was invited to Boston for a reunion of living hockey legends. Among the celebrities was Punch Broadbent, another tough customer who had been a thorn in Joliat's side throughout their playing days.

In the press room prior to the dinner, the two oldtimers became embroiled in an argument over an incident that had occurred in a game played back in the '20s. Soon they were nose to nose and their voices, raised in anger, silenced the other conversations in the room. Then punches were thrown and a dandy fight developed. Finally, scratched and bleeding, the two old adversaries were pulled apart by half a dozen bystanders. They were marched off to their rooms and told to cool off and behave themselves. But the fight wasn't over. Moments later Joliat barged into Broadbent's room, flew at him with clenched fists, and round two was underway. Once again the peacemakers came running.

Finally, stated Galloway, NHL president Clarence Campbell was called and persuaded the two legends of the game to call a truce. By then they were so battered and bruised Campbell barred them from a group photo of the celebrities and told them to forget about attending the dinner that night. "Order room service and we'll pay for it," he barked as he departed. The following morning, Joliat was seen roaming the hotel lobby. "I'm looking for my old pal Broadbent," he told acquaintances. "I'd like to buy him breakfast, or better still, a few beers if we can find a bar that's open."

Not long after the Boston shenanigans, Joliat told Ottawa sports columnist Earl McRae he'd like to make a comeback in the NHL. "If a team made me the right offer I'd come back," he said straight-faced. "I'd show 'em."

"How long do you think you'd last out there?" McRae asked.

"About five minutes."

"Only five minutes a game?"

"Game hell—five minutes a shift!"

Forum Site of Longest Game

On the night of March 23, 1936, goaltenders Norm Smith of Detroit and Lorne Chabot of the Maroons faced each other on the Forum ice in the first game of the Stanley Cup semifinals. The two netminders were about to become key performers in a remarkable playoff game, the longest one ever played.

Goalie Smith of the Wings was an ordinary guy with an ordinary name. His final NHL stats were ordinary too (81 wins and 83 losses in 199 regular-season games) but in playoff competition he sizzled. In 12 playoff starts, he won nine, lost two, earned three shutouts, and recorded a 1.23 goals-against average. His most famous shutout took place that March night at the Forum. People still talk about it—60 years later. It was the year Toe Blake was a rookie, scoring one goal in 13 games for the Canadiens.

As a teenager, Smith, a Toronto native, had switched from forward to goaltender, after quitting the game altogether for a five-year span. He jumped from an obscure Toronto industrial league to the pros, playing first with the Maroons, then the Red Wings.

In 1936 the Red Wings were still seeking their first Stanley Cup and they were underdogs against the mighty Maroons. On that March night they would play almost three full games or nine periods of gruelling hockey before taking a leg up in the series. And it was goalie Smith and a low-scoring forward named Modere "Mud" Bruneteau who emerged as Red Wing heroes in the 1–0 victory.

Smith thwarted countless Maroon attacks with fabulous goaltending. His saves bordered on the unbelievable. At the other end, Lorne Chabot was less industrious but just as invincible. Then, with four minutes to play in the sixth overtime period, Bruneteau, a two-goal scorer (with no assists) during the regular season, snapped a 25-footer past Chabot and the game was mercifully over. Detroit 1, Maroons 0.

To put Smith's feat in perspective, note that he stopped 91 shots over nine periods under tremendous playoff pressure. After the match, he staggered into the night, found a nearby pub, and almost collapsed on the floor while imbibing a couple of beers. "It wasn't the suds that did me in," he explained. "I was totally exhausted and could barely stand up."

Smith's winning effort gave the Red Wings a huge lift. They went on to upset the Maroons, the defending Cup champions, in three straight games. Incredibly, Smith registered a second consecutive shutout in game two (248 scoreless minutes) and allowed just one goal in the third game. In the best-of-five finals, the Wings whipped Toronto three games to one and skated off with their first Stanley Cup.

Smith came back the following season to lead Detroit to another Stanley Cup victory, although he was injured in game one of the finals and was replaced by Earl Robertson. He won his only Vezina trophy in '37 and was named to the NHL's first All-Star team. A severe elbow injury ended his NHL career prematurely.

While the longest-game victory ranks as Smith's greatest thrill, some of his favourite hockey memories were of games played in Quebec City.

"Oh, there were some bizarre happenings in Quebec," he recalled. "There were holes in the roof of the old arena there and the pigeons would fly in to keep warm. They'd nest in the rafters over your head so you'd be safer wearing a cap on your head. Then the fans would throw peanuts on the ice in front of me. When the play went to the other end, the pigeons would swoop down and grab the peanuts. It was distracting. I had to keep chasing them away."

Montrealers Pay Tribute to the Magnificent Morenz

"To the hockey palace his fame helped to build and where he knew his greatest triumphs, the body of Howie Morenz was taken today for public funeral services."

So began one newspaper account of the unique funeral of a gallant hockey star—Howie Morenz. The place was the Montreal Forum. The date was March 11, 1937.

"Howie will lie over the centre ice circle, guarded by his teammates and the men he first broke into professional hockey with 15 years ago. In that circle Morenz countless times had faced off the puck and cannonaded down the rink with the speed and skill that made him one of the game's greatest."

At the Forum, jammed to capacity with his devoted fans, Morenz's flower-banked bier was passed by a seemingly endless line of fans and friends. Many wiped tears from their eyes as they came to pay their respects to a magnificent athlete. Banked along the walls were floral tributes from near and far. There were even floral "sevens"—his uniform number, a numeral that, in retirement, would never grace the back of any other Canadien. There were also two floral hockey sticks. One was from the "boys in the balcony" at the Boston Garden, fans who had jeered him and grudgingly cheered him. The other was from Joe Choquette, who lovingly made the sticks Morenz played with.

When asked to comment, Canadiens manager Cecil Hart sobbed, "It's just terrible. I can't talk about it. I have known and loved him since I first signed him to a Canadiens' contract in 1922."

"No one can ever take his place with us," said Aurel Joliat, his tiny linemate.

"He was the greatest of all time," lamented Leaf coach Dick Irvin, "and the world of hockey will seem bereft without him."

Toronto owner Conn Smythe said, "The news is so shocking I can hardly credit it. I guess the old machine, one of the grandest hearts ever fabricated in a hockey frame, just broke up. He will be missed by hockey men everywhere. To Canadiens it comes as a paralyzing blow."

While his body lay in state, while young and old shuffled quietly past his resting place to view one final time the still features of hockey's greatest hero, fans in other arenas both large and small paused to reflect on the deeds of the departed Morenz. In Boston, New York, Vancouver, and Winnipeg—and Stratford, Ontario, his old hometown—the roll of muffled drums was heard. Chins dropped to chests as people stood in silence, each acutely aware that a red-shirted, balding superstar had somehow captured a piece of their heart.

Earlier in the 1936–37 season, on January 28, Montreal's 6–5 victory over Chicago had been overshadowed by an alarming incident in the first period. Morenz darted after a puck and was bodychecked by Earl Seibert. The former's skate blade caught in a crack in the boards, and with his skate embedded there, Morenz's leg twisted around and snapped with a crack that could be heard throughout the arena. He went down, writhing in pain. In an instant his season was over—and almost surely his career as well.

Earl Seibert, the six-foot-three Blackhawk defenceman, a gentle giant who would become a Hall-of-Famer, shouldered the blame for the Morenz tragedy. "I was the guy who killed him," he said. "I didn't mean to hurt him but I gave him the bodycheck. I pinned him to the boards when his skate got caught and he fell. I was stunned when I heard he'd died. I simply couldn't believe it. He was the greatest all-round player in the game." Seibert was absolved of all blame and did not receive a penalty on the play.

So highly regarded was Morenz that a rival coach once ordered his players not to hit him during a game. In New York one night, Morenz skated out to face the Rangers. New York coach Lester Patrick admonished his players: "Don't hit Morenz tonight. The little guy is nursing a leg so sore he shouldn't be playing. He only dressed because he knows the New York fans are anxious to see him perform. So get in his way but go easy on him and his gimpy leg."

For 14 years Morenz was one of the most dynamic figures in the game. He scored 270 career goals, and with Aurel Joliat and Johnny Gagnon as his wingmates he soared to unparalleled hockey heights.

A Writer Mourns Morenz

On the day after Morenz's sudden death, Andy Lytle wrote an obituary in the *Toronto Star*:

> *Like a tired child dropping softly to sleep, Howie Morenz died in a Montreal hospital last night.*
>
> *Morenz, the flashing meteor of the ice lanes, the little man who proved that "they do come back from the valley of regret and disillusion," ate a light supper, smiled at his nurse and then turned his head wearily on the pillow as though to fall asleep.*
>
> *The watching nurse, noting the strange pallor settling over his face, called a doctor. But before the medical man arrived the turbulent soul of one of the greatest figures that ever laced on skates had found eternal peace.*
>
> *It was his heart that gave out, the experts said sorrowfully. To those who knew the strong vein of sentimentality that surged in the make-up of this remarkable athlete it was as if the fibre of the man slowly disintegrated as he faced the uncertainties of a hockeyless future.*
>
> *A crestfallen Morenz had come back to Canadiens this season after a season on foreign ice with Chicago and then with Rangers.*
>
> *In a few months he had re-scaled the heights. Was once more the flashing, dashing Morenz, the streak of Stratford, the beloved of the hockey gods who sit in silence or roar like maddened souls during the progress of the games in Montreal.*
>
> *Then a quick twist, a fall on the ice and Morenz was carried away, his leg broken in two or three places.*
>
> *As he recovered slowly, Morenz held court in his hospital ward. His friends were legion, his admirers more. They called to see him, to talk, to commiserate and to secure his autograph.*

Howie again broke under the strain and the excitement of this renewed adoration. Last weekend the doctors belatedly clamped on the lid. No more visitors, no more chats. He was, the experts said, on the verge of a complete nervous breakdown. The strain was too great.

And then, a few days later, as his friends looked confidently forward to his complete recovery, with the unexpectedness of a bolt of lightning from a cloudless sky, the weary, exhausted figure heaved a tired sigh and turned his face to the wall.

A moment later, to a startled world and to his agonized people, the tragic words were spoken—"Howie Morenz is dead." It was his brave heart that had given suddenly, tragically out, his doctors said.

Morenz is survived by Mrs. Morenz and three children. Howie Jr., 10, skating mascot of the Canadiens, Donald, 4, and Marlene, 3.

Marlene Morenz grew up and married Bernie "Boom Boom" Geoffrion, a hockey star who surpassed the goal-scoring record of his illustrious father-in-law, 393 goals to 270. But Geoffrion played in 883 games to Howie's 550. Howie's goals-per-game average marginally exceeded his son-in-law's: 0.4909 to 0.4451.

The Man Who Checked Morenz Never Recovered

On May 22, 1990, in the little town of Agawan, Massachusetts, Earl Seibert was buried. One of the greatest defencemen in the history of hockey was laid to rest and not a single representative from the hockey establishment was there to bid the 78-year-old cancer-stricken hockey legend farewell.

Between 1935 and 1944, the strapping Kitchener native made the NHL All-Star team ten consecutive times. But one night in 1937, Chicago's Seibert checked Montreal's Morenz and both men's lives changed forever. Morenz suffered a broken leg and died six weeks later in hospital. Seibert was devastated at the news and carried the guilt of the Morenz tragedy to his grave.

"My father never got over it," Oliver Seibert, a son, said at the burial.

Montreal fans never forgave Seibert for his check on Morenz. Throughout the rest of his NHL career, he was vilified every time he stepped on the Forum ice surface. And when he left the game, he vanished into obscurity.

News of his passing was carried by the wire services. Therefore, family members might have anticipated the arrival of at least a handful of former teammates and NHL representatives at his funeral. When none showed up, and not even a card or floral display was received, it was a bitter disappointment to the surviving Seiberts.

Death of the Flying Dutchman

As the 1930s ended, the Canadiens found themselves mourning the loss of a popular and dynamic performer for the second time in less than three years. First it was Howie Morenz, who died in hospital in 1937. Then on August 25, 1939, Albert Charles "Babe" Siebert, the man known as the Flying Dutchman, was cut down in the prime of his life, a drowning victim in Lake Huron.

Hockey honours flowed toward Siebert from the time he broke into the NHL with the Maroons in 1925–26, when he played a key role in Montreal's Stanley Cup triumph that year, on through his glory years as a member of the Maroons' high-scoring S Line of Siebert, Nels Stewart, and Hooley Smith, and later with Boston, New York, and the Canadiens. The Flying Dutchman came late to the Flying Frenchmen, arriving for the 1936–37 season as a defenceman who'd once starred on the wing. In his three seasons with the Habs, he was a first-team All-Star twice. In his first season (1936–37), he won the Hart Trophy as the NHL's MVP, he was team captain for all three years, and he was named to coach the team for the following season. Unfortunately, an off-season tragedy prevented him from filling that position.

Siebert showed the world a pair of personalities. On the ice he was a roaring, driven demon who enraged opponents and angered teammates with his verbal outbursts. Former NHL defenceman Bill "Flash" Hollett, now 85, said recently, "Siebert wouldn't just cut you down. He'd send you right to the hospital." After games Siebert became a quiet, solemn figure who smoked his cigarettes and melted into the background. He would disappear quickly from the room because he had other duties to perform. He would stride back to rinkside where his invalid wife was waiting. He would kiss her gently on the cheek, then lift her in his strong arms and take her outside where a car waited. He would deposit her gently inside and they would go home to their children, kiddies who adored their giant of a father and their frail mother.

She had become a helpless invalid after the second Siebert child was born, and medical expenses consumed every penny of Siebert's salary. With no money to pay a housekeeper or a maid, Babe did all the cooking and the housework and always provided the tender, loving care so necessary to the little ones and their mother. Little wonder that in the Siebert household, three sets of eyes looked adoringly on the husband and father who devoted himself to their well-being. When he went on road trips with the hockey team, friends and neighbours volunteered to handle his household duties.

The arena was the ideal place to seek relief from his frustrations and his anger. He would bellow, snarl, and roar, igniting the crowd with his bruising style of play. That was Siebert the hardened hockey hero. But much more heroic were the deeds he performed without fanfare each day in the confines of his small home.

An All-Star game was played in Babe's memory in Montreal on October 29, 1939. A sum of $10,000 from the proceeds was turned over to Siebert's widow and children.

Chapter 4
THE IRVIN ERA

Irvin's Gashouse Gang

Dick Irvin the coach once said, "In all my years of hockey, I've never encountered any players like the ones I coached in Montreal from 1943 to 1946. They were my Gashouse Gang, a slambang bunch of men who could out-bump, out-fight and out-score any team in sight. As a coach, it was a breeze. I would simply open the gate and say 'Sic 'em!' In the 1943–44 season we lost only five games. In the playoffs we lost the opener, then won eight straight to grab the Cup."

Irvin always insisted his "Punch Line" of Rocket Richard, Toe Blake, and Elmer Lach was the greatest line in hockey history. "They had everything," he would declare. "Courage, competitive fire and tremendous class. They performed like a smooth running machine. No line was any better. My, but they were tough and talented.

"Toe Blake was one of the toughest of the old pros on my roster. Toe injured his tailbone one time and was in such pain he couldn't even sit on the bench. Finally our trainer filled a cushion with air for him to perch on. Even then, there was such agony on his face that I was about to send him to the dressing room. Just then the Leafs tied the score and Blake roared, 'Let me out there!' Before I could answer he'd jumped over the boards and shot into the action. Moments later he whistled a pass to Elmer [Lach] and they combined for the winning goal.

"Ken Reardon and Murph Chamberlain were also tops when it came to toughness. Reardon always preferred to go right through a man rather than around him—blasting his way from end to end. During the 1945 playoffs we had to encase Chamberlain in rolls of adhesive to protect his broken ribs. When the adhesive hindered his breathing, he stripped it off and proceeded to bump the Bruins until their legs buckled.

"Here's a funny story about Chamberlain. One day at practice I put a board in the middle of the net. It was a reminder that the players should be shooting for the corners. Murph's wife happened to be at the practice that day and when it was over she said, 'Wasn't Murph wonderful. He hit that board every time.'"

Irvin had great respect for Tommy Gorman, the Montreal manager during the Gashouse era. "I had worked for Smythe in Toronto and McLaughlin in Chicago, men who put the fear of God in everybody around them, so it was a shock to come to Montreal and work for somebody who didn't go around with a whip in his hand. One morning I put the players through a brutal workout, even though we had won a game the night before. I tongue-lashed them and told them they'd won on luck, not effort and they should be ashamed of themselves. Just as I finished, Tommy Gorman entered the room and bounced from player to player, pounding each man on the back. 'Great game last night! Attaboy! A wonderful victory! You've never looked better!'

"I glanced around the room and the players were trying to stifle their laughter. When I failed to hold back a grin, they all broke up. We roared with mirth while Gorman stood there looking totally confused."

Former referee Bill Chadwick once said, "Dick Irvin was the best coach in the NHL when I was involved in the game. He was everything you could ask for in a coach. He lived, ate and slept hockey and he was also the cleanest man in the game. Why? Because on road trips he filled his pockets with those little packets of soap from the hotel rooms he stayed in. He was a great hockey man and his NHL record confirms it."

Perhaps the most interesting aspect of Tommy Gorman's long career in hockey was his ability to win the Stanley Cup as manager or coach wherever he turned up. He captured it with the Ottawa Senators three times in the early '20s. In 1934 he guided the Chicago Blackhawks to the Cup, only to be fired. He surfaced with the Montreal Maroons a year later and won another title. His final Cup victories were in Montreal with the Canadiens in 1944 and 1946.

Dick Irvin: Great Player, Great Coach

In 1913, as an amateur player with the Winnipeg Monarchs, Dick Irvin once scored nine goals in a senior-hockey game. Irvin's Monarchs won the game over a strong Toronto team 9–1. His remarkable scoring outburst earned Irvin a place in Ripley's popular "Believe It or Not" syndicated newspaper column. A year later his inspired play for the Monarchs brought Winnipeg the Canadian senior championship and the Allan Cup.

He moved on to Regina, then to Portland of the Pacific Coast Hockey League. In 1925–26 the Portland Rosebuds (How many hockey teams have been called the Rosebuds?) were sold intact to Chicago interests and became the Blackhawks of the NHL. Irvin played brilliantly for Chicago and finished second in the scoring race in 1926–27, a point behind Bill Cook of the Rangers and four points ahead of Howie Morenz. Early in his second season as a Blackhawk, Irvin was slammed to the ice by husky Red Dutton. Irvin suffered a fractured skull, recovered sufficiently to play in 39 games the following season, and then decided that his playing days were over.

When Chicago won a mere seven games in each of those two seasons, and finished 30 points behind Boston, the American Division leaders, in 1929–30, Irvin was called on to coach the team of non-achievers. He was a natural behind the bench. The Hawks improved remarkably and won

24 games in 1930–31. One of Irvin's innovations was to throw three fresh forward lines at the opposition in short shifts. That season the Hawks won playoff series from Toronto and the Rangers before bowing to the Habs in the Stanley Cup finals.

When the Hawks inexplicably dropped him following his impressive coaching debut, Toronto's Conn Smythe snapped him up after the Leafs stumbled through the opening games of the 1931–32 season. Irvin led the Leafs to a Stanley Cup triumph that season, a fitting way to celebrate the inaugural year of Maple Leaf Gardens.

After nine seasons with the Leafs, Irvin moved on to Montreal, where the Canadiens' fortunes had hit a new low. It wasn't long before he moulded a winning combination, guiding the Habs to Cup wins in 1944, 1946, and 1953. His 1943–44 team lost only five games out of 50 and established a team-record winning percentage of .830. His club went 13 games into the season before tasting defeat and later won 13 consecutive games at home. On November 21, 1943, the Habs rocked Boston 13–4, tallying 35 scoring points in the game. On February 6, 1943, Elmer Lach recorded six assists in a game (8–3 over Boston), and on December 28, 1944, Rocket Richard collected eight points in a game (9–1 over Detroit). All of the preceding are long-standing team records, although the Rocket's eight-point mark was later tied (in 1954) by Bert Olmstead.

Incredibly, Irvin's Habs completed the 1943–44 season without losing a single one of 25 home encounters, and the following season they lost just two on Forum ice. Two defeats in 50 home games would elevate most coaches onto a cloud bearing the Rocket's number. Irvin probably searched long and hard for reasons the two games were lost.

In 1946 Irvin's Canadiens defeated Boston in the finals four games to one. Elmer Lach led all playoff scorers, with 17 points in nine games. In 1953 Irvin called on Jacques Plante to replace Gerry McNeil in the Montreal net and Plante responded with a glittering 1.75 goals-against average in four games as the Habs ousted the Bruins in the finals. Again, Montreal's margin was four games to one.

Irvin finished his great coaching career back in Chicago in 1955–56, taking over a club that had finished in the NHL basement for seven of the previous nine years. Before he could begin one of his patented rebuilding jobs, he was forced to deal with a personal challenge, a lengthy battle with cancer which he was unable to win. He died in Montreal in May of 1957.

Irvin missed the playoffs only twice in 27 seasons and passed along his gift for language, his love of the game, and his fascination for hockey statistics to his son Dick, Junior. In his final coaching season, Irvin told a *Sports Illustrated* reporter that he knew exactly how many NHL goals he'd seen: 8,705. "My players have scored 4,721 goals and been scored on 3,984 times." He followed up by telling the astonished scribe that his hockey travels had carried him over 1,050,000 miles—most of it by train. At the time he reigned as hockey's winningest coach. Today he ranks third in coaching wins, behind Scotty Bowman and Al Arbour.

With the Canadiens, one of the highlights of Irvin's annual training camp was the scrimmage he supervised on the final day. He would order a full-length intersquad game, pitting the rookies against the veterans. He'd visit the veterans' dressing room and bark at them, "Fellows, there's an eager bunch of youngsters in the next room dying to take your jobs away. Are you going to let them push you aside?" Then he'd lecture the rookies, "Listen, I've only got room on my club for two or three of you and today's the day I decide who sticks. A lot depends on who can go out there and knock the Rocket or big Bouchard flat on his arse."

Those games were often more entertaining than the regular-season match-ups. When Montrealers heard what sounded like the cannon shots echoing off Mount Royal, they'd nod wisely and tell bystanders, worried perhaps that another war had broken out, "No, it's just Dick Irvin's last training-camp game."

Asked about such do-or-die confrontations, Irvin would simply smile and say, "It may sound mean, it may sound brutal, but it seemed to work. Some kids earned their ticket to the NHL by busting their arse in that final day of camp."

Five for the Rocket

On March 23, 1944, Maurice Richard went on a scoring rampage against the Toronto Maple Leafs in a Stanley Cup playoff game at the Forum. The Leafs had finished a dismal third in the NHL standings that spring, 33 points behind the Habs, who lost a mere five games all season. So it infuriated Dick Irvin's charges when the Leafs stunned Montreal 3–1 in the series opener.

In game two, at the Forum, the Rocket was checked closely by Toronto's Bob Davidson during the first period. In the second period Richard shook away from Davidson and scored three goals. In the third period the Rocket whipped in two more and Montreal evened the series with a 5–1 triumph.

Over the years Davidson has been unfairly criticized for not checking Richard more closely. Recently he told me, "First of all, Rocket only got away from me for three of those goals. Dick Irvin played Richard on different lines that night and on a pair of his goals some of my teammates were supposed to be looking after him.

"And on his first goal, I have to laugh. I had him pinned right up to the boards and he was trying to push me away. There was no way I was going to let him go. Then a fan at rinkside reached out and grabbed my stick. Yanked it right out of my hands. Remember, there was no protective glass along the side boards in those days. Well, I thought Bill Chadwick, the referee, would blow his whistle and let me go to the bench for a new stick. But he didn't. Rocket, meanwhile, twisted away, grabbed the loose puck, and went in and scored."

Veteran sportswriter Elmer Ferguson, who was asked to pick the three stars that night, jolted the Forum crowd when his third-star selection was announced.

"Tonight's third star—Maurice Ree-chaaard!" said the public-address announcer.

The fans murmured their protest. How could Ferguson pick Richard as third star when he'd scored all of his team's goals? There couldn't possibly be two players on the ice who'd outshone him.

"Tonight's second star—Maurice Ree-chaaard!" the man continued.

Now the fans understood what Fergie was up to. They began to applaud wildly.

"And tonight's number-one star—Maurice Ree-chaaard!"

Thousands of ear drums were all but punctured from the roar that filled the Forum.

It was the first (and only) time one player captured all three stars. Ferguson later selected that game as the most memorable he ever witnessed. Bob Davidson, one of hockey's toughest checkers, thought it memorable too, but for different reasons.

The last time a player scored five or more goals in a playoff game was back in 1917 when Bernie Morris of Seattle potted six goals against the Canadiens.

Referee Chadwick would later say of Richard, "The Rocket was in a class by himself as a hockey player, especially in the playoffs. He had a nose for the net and from the blue line in he would explode. If his team needed a big goal, the Rocket would get it, and he'd practically take somebody's eye out to do it.

"Rocket was a mean guy on and off the ice. I don't think he ever had a good thing to say about anybody. And he could never control himself. He'd go wild when he got too emotional. His eyes would light up like goal lights. There was a raging fire inside him like I've never seen in another player."

Blake Shines in '44 Cup Triumph

Hector "Toe" Blake brought much glory to the Canadiens as a player and coach. One of his personal highs as a playoff performer took place in the spring of 1944, when he sparked Montreal to a 5–4 overtime victory over Chicago in the fourth and final game of the Stanley Cup finals. The Habs trailed by three goals in the final period of game four when Blake went to work, setting up the plays that led to three straight Montreal goals and a tie score. Then, after nine minutes of overtime, he slapped in the game-winner as 12,880 fans roared their appreciation. Blake's five-point night gave him a new playoff-points record of 18 and the win topped Montreal's most successful season ever. Aside from winning eight straight playoff games over Toronto and Chicago, they set a new scoring mark of 234 goals and a regular-season point record of 83.

The Rocket Set the Standard

When Rocket Richard potted 50 goals in 50 games during the 1944–45 NHL season, Montreal fans marvelled at the feat. They had never seen a player with such a scoring touch, nor had they witnessed such a productive line as the trio of Richard, Elmer Lach, and Hector "Toe" Blake. The trio were aptly named the "Punch Line." The line averaged 4.4 points per game, a record that has never been matched, and they finished one-two-three in the individual scoring race. Lach collected 80 points, Richard 73, and Blake 67. The Habs finished in first place with 80 points and lost only eight games all season.

But it was Richard's desperate attempt to garner 50 goals in a like number of games that captured the headlines. And he did it, as he did most things on the ice, in spectacular style, delivering his bombshell in the third period of the final game, just as the final seconds were being swept off the clock at the Boston Garden. His 50th was the fourth goal in Montreal's 4–2 victory over the Bruins, the final goal in Montreal's season.

Today, at age 76, Richard draws a blank when he tries to recall the milestone marker. "I just don't remember how it was scored," he confesses.

However, the victim of his history-making goal, former Boston goalie Harvey Bennett, remembers it well. "Elmer Lach gave him a hell of a lot of help on the play," Bennett, now 70, told the *Hockey News* recently. "In fact, Elmer knocked me on my ass and when I was down and out, bang, Richard whipped it in the net."

The historic goal was scored on March 18, at 17:45 of the third period, 135 seconds from the end of the season.

Richard added another six goals in six playoff games, for a total of 56 goals in 56 games. But his finest personal season ended on a sour note when the Leafs upset the Habs four games to two in the Stanley Cup semifinals.

Richard, Blake, and Lach earned berths on the 1944–45 first All-Star team, as did the Habs' Butch Bouchard on defence and Bill Durnan in goal. It was a season when the Canadiens, led by the Rocket, were odds-on to win the Stanley Cup. But rookie goalie Frank McCool and the Leafs stunned them in the playoffs.

Durnan's Shutout Streak

Bill Durnan, the ambidextrous netminder, still holds a modern-day record for shutout minutes that may last well into the next century. Or even forever. His mark reads "Longest shutout sequence by a goaltender…309 minutes, 21 seconds." He set the record during the 1948–49 season.

From the moment Roy Conacher of the Blackhawks scored against him at 16:15 of the first period on February 24, 1949, to the 5:36 mark of the second period on March 9, Durnan stymied the greatest marksmen in the game. Curiously, the streak started in the Chicago Stadium and it ended there too.

Two nights after allowing Conacher's goal, Durnan blanked the Detroit Red Wings 1–0. Four nights later he shut out Toronto 2–0 at Maple Leaf Gardens. The following weekend he mesmerized the Boston Bruins in a home-and-home series, 4–0 at the Forum and 1–0 back in Boston.

It added up to five hours, nine minutes, and 21 seconds of scoreless goaltending. In the four games, Durnan turned back 95 shots. His best performance in the four games was in Boston, where the fans gave him a standing ovation at the final whistle.

In the streak-ending game in Chicago on March 9, it appeared as though Durnan would record his fifth consecutive shutout. Montreal was leading 2–0 in the second period when Gaye Stewart of the Blackhawks shot the puck through Durnan's legs. Durnan got a piece of it, but not enough, and the red light flashed behind him.

"Instead of celebrating his goal, Stewart skated over to me and told me how sorry he was the streak was over," Durnan said. "I had to chuckle over that because, in a way, I was relieved to get it behind me."

Durnan won the Vezina Trophy that season, and every season he played for Montreal except one: 1947–48.

In 1950, the season following his four-game shutout streak, Durnan walked away from hockey. "I could never stand another season of goaltending," he told general manager Frank Selke. "My nerves are all shot. I'm through with hockey."

Smythe Loved the Rocket

On his 50th birthday Toronto Maple Leaf owner Conn Smythe decided to journey to Montreal to see his first hockey game in months. He'd been badly injured during his army service overseas and ever since his return to Canada he'd been confined to his bedroom, where he conducted his business on the telephone. On the eve of his birthday, he decided he was well enough to journey to Montreal to watch the Canadiens host Chicago. The following day he would attend a meeting of the NHL governors. The game he saw was an outstanding one, a 1–1 tie. Montreal's lone goal was scored by Maurice Richard, who bullied his way in from the blue line with two Chicago defenders draped all over him.

Smythe couldn't get the image of Richard's goal out of his mind. He returned to Toronto and accosted his assistant, Frank Selke: "What's this you've been telling me about wartime hockey being second rate? That Richard kid I saw at the Forum scored as pretty a goal as I've ever seen. We've got to try and land him for the Leafs." Smythe offered the Canadiens $25,000 for Richard, a sum that made Montreal management laugh. "Sorry, Mr. Smythe, no amount of money can buy the Rocket," was the reply.

It was due to Richard that Smythe uttered one of his most-quoted phrases. The Rocket was involved in a wild fight with the Leafs' Bob Bailey one night at Maple Leaf Gardens. Asked about the battle, Smythe said, "We've got to stamp out that kind of thing or people are going to keep on buying tickets."

Even though he admired the Rocket tremendously, it didn't prevent Smythe from sending verbal darts in his direction whenever the Leafs met Montreal. One night at the Forum, Smythe found himself seated right next to Richard's mother-in-law. They argued and snarled at each other all through the game. Late in the contest, when tempers cooled a little, Smythe asked her what she had been saying to him in French. She laughed and replied, "That's where I have the advantage, Mr. Smythe. I can tell you what a blankety-blank you are in two languages."

One for the Book

Ever hear of Eddie Emberg, Montreal Canadien? Nobody else has either. But Emberg's name is in the NHL annals as the lone player to score a Stanley Cup playoff goal without ever appearing in a regular-season game.

It happened in 1945, when Emberg was summoned from the Quebec Senior Hockey League for two playoff games against Toronto. He scored his only NHL goal in one of the games, a 10–3 win over the Leafs.

Riot at the Forum

On March 17, 1955, shortly after 9 p.m., an unknown spectator lobbed a tear-gas bomb into the lower-level seats at the Montreal Forum. Over 16,000 fans were watching the game between Detroit and the Canadiens that night—actually, most of them were watching one man at the game, league president Clarence Campbell—and they were barely aware that Detroit had coasted to a 4–1 lead when the bomb went off.

Campbell, accompanied by his secretary, Phyllis King (later his wife), arrived at the Forum almost 15 minutes after the opening whistle. When he strolled to his seat, the crowd stood and booed his every step. Then came the missiles: programs, peanuts, toe rubbers, coins, an egg. As the objects rained down on him, he sat stoically and tried to ignore them. He even smiled once or twice.

He had been warned to stay away. During the past 24 hours his office staff had been deluged with phone calls. One caller had shouted, "When I catch up to him, I will kill him!" A woman had warned him, "Don't show up at the next hockey game or you'll be murdered." A man called to say he'd plant a bomb in Campbell's office and blow him to smithereens.

There were extra police on duty at the Forum that night but few, if any, appeared willing to protect Campbell from the howling mob.

Everyone in Canada knew why Campbell had suddenly become the most detested man in the province of Quebec. An explosion of mob fury should have been anticipated the moment he set foot in the Forum. On the previous day, the league president had suspended Maurice "Rocket" Richard, the idol of all of French Canada, for attacking a Boston player and a game official during a match at the Boston Garden four days earlier. The suspension—not for a game or two, but for the rest of the season *and the entire playoffs*—had shocked Montrealers and triggered an outburst of hysteria and unbelievable animosity toward the stern-faced Campbell.

No matter that the fiery Richard, never one to shy away from confrontation on the ice, had been in Campbell's court several times before. No matter that he'd paid more fines ($2,500) than any other player in league history. For him to miss the playoffs was unthinkable, intolerable, and a calamity. In the minds of Montrealers, Richard *was* the playoffs. A suspension also meant he'd lose the NHL scoring title to teammate Bernard Geoffrion, a poor imitation of the Rocket. At age 33, it might be Richard's last opportunity to win the Art Ross Trophy. Campbell was a cad. His decision was preposterous and so unfair. His cruelty was unforgivable. Surely it was another example of an Anglo punishing a French Canadian. "If the Rocket's last name was Richardson, he'd have received a slap on the wrist," wrote one reporter.

In far-off Detroit, Ted Lindsay, who'd tangled often with the Rocket, dumped fuel on the fire. "He should have been suspended for life," snarled Terrible Ted. Others, none of them Richard fans and none living in Quebec, supported Campbell's decision to ban the Rocket.

At the Forum, in the closing moments of the first period, a young man bullied his way past an usher and attacked the NHL chief. He lashed out twice with his fists before the ushers could intervene. When the period ended, another wild-eyed fan rushed in and squashed two tomatoes on Campbell's chest.

Hugh MacLennan, the well-known Canadian writer, was sitting a few rows in front of Campbell. He would say later, "To understand the feelings of the crowd that night is to understand a good bit of the social conditions of Quebec of the 1950s." He would add, "I remember knowing with very frightening and distinct certainty that with the mood of the mob, anything could happen."

When the tear-gas bomb went off about eight or ten metres away from where Campbell was sitting, sending a cloud of smoke in the air, everyone reacted. Fans bolted from their seats and headed for the exits. Most covered their faces with gloves and scarves. Campbell leaped up and fought his way through the crowd to the Forum clinic, where he huddled with fire department officials. After a brief, animated discussion, a decision was made to clear the building. And Campbell made another decision—to forfeit the game to Detroit. At that point in the contest, the Red Wings were leading 4–1.

Jacques Belanger, the public-address announcer, ordered the spectators to stay calm and move quickly to the exits. He reminded them to keep their ticket stubs. Meanwhile the organist kept busy but few could hear him over the roar of the crowd. Fortunately there was no real panic, otherwise hundreds might have been trampled in the stampede.

Outside the Forum, a crowd of several thousand gathered. Many were hoodlums and demonstrators without tickets to the match. They began throwing missiles, which scarred the brickwork of the building and shattered windows. Some smashed the windows of nearby streetcars and pulled their cables off the overhead wires, stalling traffic in all directions. People with blood flowing down their faces were loaded into police cars that pushed their way through the throng.

The angry mob moved along St. Catherine Street. Cars were overturned, a newspaper stand was set afire, and bricks and bottles were tossed through shop windows. Looters snatched up valuable merchandise. Dozens of fans, wild for revenge against Campbell, were arrested and hauled away.

Many of them were teenagers. Less than 250 policemen faced a howling mob of over 10,000 and order was not restored until after 3 a.m.

"Can you imagine fans rioting over a suspension in any other city?" Dick Irvin asked recently. "Would they riot in the streets if a star athlete in baseball or basketball was suspended? Of course not. But the Rocket's suspension—that was something else."

Before the Red Wings left the city, manager Jack Adams delivered a parting shot: "You newspapermen have turned Richard into an idol, a man whose suspension can turn fans into shrieking idiots. Now hear this: Richard is no hero. He let his team down, he let hockey down, he let the public down."

The following day, Richard, who had watched the uproar from his rinkside seat, pleaded with his fans to stay calm. He seldom discusses the event today, except to say, "It was Mr. Campbell who incited the fans. If he had not gone to the game that night..."

Richard lost the scoring crown to Boom Boom Geoffrion that spring, by a single point. Many fans unfairly blamed Geoffrion for not passing up scoring opportunities in the handful of games that remained so that Richard could be the winner.

The ugly incident, often called *L'affaire Richard*, was blamed for the elimination of the Habs from the 1955 playoffs. With their star player sidelined, with Beliveau battling an illness, and with their emotions still in turmoil, the Habs were beaten by the Detroit Red Wings in the finals. The Red Wings captured the first two games on home ice, establishing a record for consecutive victories (15), and they also won game seven at the Olympia, where they had not been defeated since December 19, 1954.

The Habs, to their credit, stayed on the ice to congratulate the new champions and Red Wings president Marguerite Norris. The previous year the Canadiens had snubbed the winners and had been criticized in the press for their poor sportsmanship.

Oldtime Montreal fans still deal in "ifs." "If" Richard had stayed out of trouble, "if" his punishment had been less severe, "if" the decision hadn't affected the entire team, the Habs, not the Red Wings, might have won the Stanley Cup.

And "if" they had? The record book shows that Montreal, the following season, began a string of five consecutive Cup victories.

It should have been six in a row, argue the oldtimers. Such a tragedy. And it was all the fault of that man Campbell.

What Happened in Boston

No executive in any sport was more vilified than NHL president Clarence Campbell in the spring of 1955. He was assaulted and abused, and received several death threats when fans of Maurice "Rocket" Richard reacted with fury to the suspension of their idol after an on-ice incident during a game in Boston.

On March 16, 1955, a hearing was held at the NHL offices in Montreal to ascertain what really happened in Boston. After scrutinizing reports from the game officials, and after listening to explanations from both Richard and Hal Laycoe of the Boston Bruins and other witnesses, officials concluded the following:

At about the 14-minute mark of the third period, when Boston was playing a man short and the Canadiens had removed their goalkeeper for a sixth attacker (an odd strategy with so much time remaining), Richard was proceeding over the Boston blue line. As Richard skated past Hal Laycoe, the latter high-sticked him on the side of the head. The referee promptly and visibly signalled a penalty to Laycoe but permitted the play to continue as the Canadiens were still in possession of the puck.

Richard skated around the Boston goal and back almost to the blue line when the whistle blew. Richard rubbed his hand on his head and indicated to the referee that he had been injured. Suddenly he skated toward Laycoe, who was a short distance away, and, swinging his stick over his head with both hands, he struck Laycoe a blow on the shoulder and face. At the time Laycoe was struck, he had dropped his stick and gloves.

The linesmen grabbed the two players and Richard's stick was taken away from him. However, he was able to break away from linesman Thompson, and, picking up a loose stick, again attacked Laycoe with two one-handed swings, striking him over the back and breaking the stick. Again linesman Thompson got a grip on Richard but the Montreal player was able to get away. Somehow the Rocket found another stick and struck Laycoe a third time across the back as the Bruin ducked to avoid the blow.

Linesman Thompson again restrained Richard. This time he forced the Rocket to the ice and held him there until a Montreal player pushed Thompson away, allowing Richard to scramble to his feet. He was seething with anger and lashed out at Thompson, striking him in the face with two hard blows.

Thompson finally got Richard under control and signalled for the Canadiens trainer to come and escort Richard to the first-aid room, where he received four or five stitches on the left side of his head.

Referee Frank Udvari handed a match penalty to Richard for deliberately injuring Laycoe and a five-minute penalty to Laycoe for high-sticking Richard, causing the head wound.

At the penalty box, Udvari ordered Laycoe to take a seat—inside the box. When he failed to do so, the Bruin was assessed a further ten-minute misconduct penalty. When he finally entered the box, Laycoe threw a towel at Udvari, striking him on the leg.

At the hearing in Montreal, Laycoe testified that in the original contact with Richard when the game was in progress, he had been struck a terrific blow on his glasses by Richard's stick. He immediately and instinctively hit back. Referee Udvari made no reference to this earlier blow and Richard said he did not know whether he hit Laycoe at that time or not.

Richard contended that he was dazed and did not know what he was doing because of the blow he had received on the head. He also said that when he struck the linesman in the face with his fists, he mistook him for one of the Boston players, some of whom were milling around the area.

Following the hearing, Clarence Campbell ruled that Richard be suspended for the remainder of the regular season and also for the play-offs. Compared to modern-day suspensions—Colorado's Claude Lemieux received a two-game suspension and a $1,000 fine for a cheap-shot hit from behind on an unsuspecting Chris Draper of Detroit in the 1996 play-offs, leaving Draper with a fractured jaw, a broken nose, and more than 30 stitches—Richard's punishment seems unusually harsh. It left a multitude of his supporters seething with rage.

Three weeks later, Montreal coach Dick Irvin was still steaming over the Richard suspension. During the Stanley Cup finals against Detroit, Irvin encountered linesman Sammy Babcock sitting in the lobby of the Leland Hotel in Detroit. Irvin walked directly toward Babcock and began verbally assaulting the startled official, who was the other linesman on the ice the night Richard attacked Hal Laycoe in Boston.

Pounding the air with his arms, Irvin shouted, "And what did you do? All three of you officials told Campbell that Richard was carrying the puck at the time. But at the same hearing Laycoe claimed it was he who was carrying the puck. That makes all three of you blankety-blank liars!"

Past Misdeeds of the Rocket

When NHL president Clarence Campbell suspended Rocket Richard in March 1955, he might have argued that he had long erred on the side of leniency when called upon to judge the frequent on- and off-the-ice escapades of the temperamental right winger.

Shortly after the incident, hockey writer Gord Walker reached into the newspaper archives and listed some of the turbulent episodes in which Richard was, more often than not, the central figure:

April 10, 1947: In a Stanley Cup playoff game in Montreal, Richard slashed Toronto's Vic Lynn, who was knocked unconscious and required six stitches to close a cut over his left eye. Later during the same period, Richard slashed Bill Ezinicki's head for eight stitches. The Rocket drew a major penalty for the first offence and a match penalty for the second. He was fined $250.

March 13, 1951: Richard was fined $500 for molesting referee Hugh McLean in the lobby of a New York hotel. On the night prior to the attack, Richard had been given a game misconduct penalty for fighting in the penalty box with Leo Reise. Then Richard struck linesman Eddie Mepham with his stick; New York and Boston writers protested the leniency of the decision, pointing out that Ted Lindsay and Bill Ezinicki had each been fined $300 and suspended for three games for a stick-swinging bout earlier in the season.

October 31, 1951: During a game in Toronto, Richard swung his stick at a railside spectator. After the game he swung his stick at another patron. No disciplinary action was taken.

November 1, 1951: Richard whirled his stick over his head to deter Toronto's Fern Flaman as both players raced for the puck. Both players started to fight. During the fight, Richard was seen to kick Flaman in the chest with his skate. Then he punched Bill Juzda to the ice. Richard drew two majors and a misconduct. An automatic fine of $50 accompanied the latter penalty. No league action was taken.

October 21, 1952: Richard was fined $10 and costs for assaulting a policeman at Valleyfield, Quebec, where the Canadiens played an exhibition game. He was in street clothes, nursing a groin injury, when he took exception to verbal abuse from the fans. He got into a fight and punched a policeman during the scuffle.

January 21, 1953: Detroit's Jack Adams warned Richard to "Behave—or else." Adams claimed Richard crosschecked Marcel Pronovost, knocking out two teeth. The following night Richard broke Glen Skov's nose with a board check. Richard said Adams was "full of bull" and that "I just got mad and took a run at everybody."

March 9, 1953: General John Reed Kilpatrick, president of Madison Square Garden, protested "a mere five minute penalty" to Richard after the Rocket whacked Ranger Ed Kullman over the head with his stick, slicing open his scalp for eight stitches.

December 13, 1954: Richard apologized to league president Campbell for articles ghost-written for the Rocket in a French-language newspaper. In the articles, Richard referred to Campbell as a "dictator" and said, "he smiles and openly shows pleasure when an opposing club scores against us." He suggested the league president was guilty of racial discrimination and added, "If Mr. Campbell wants to throw me out of the league for daring to criticize him, let him do it." After accepting the Rocket's apology, Campbell ordered Richard to post a $1,000 bond as evidence of good faith.

December 29, 1954: Richard charged Leaf rookie Bob Bailey and butt-ended him in the face, knocking out two teeth. He repeatedly tried to retrieve his stick to renew his attack on Bailey after the fight between them was stopped. Richard flicked his glove in the face of linesman George Hayes and refused to leave the ice when ordered to by the referee. He was fined $250.

NHL president Clarence Campbell once said, "Fines never bothered Richard. For every $250 I fined him, Quebec businessmen would send him $1,000. Richard could do no wrong in Quebec. I was always the villain."

Unlike most Habs fans, the Rocket never saw the Canadiens perform when he was growing up. There was never any money in the Richard household for such a treat and nobody ever offered to take him to a game. So the first NHL game he saw was one he played in.

On December 27, 1944, now married to Lucille, the sister of a man who coached him in minor hockey, Richard moved to new digs on Papineau Street. He worked all night and grabbed a couple of hours of sleep before reporting to the Forum. Complaining that he was "almost too tired to suit up," he went out and scored a team-record eight points (five goals and three assists) against Detroit in a 9–1 rout.

Former NHL referee Red Storey has often said, "There'll never be another Rocket, even if they're playing hockey a thousand years from now. I've played every game, reffed a few thousand and seen a lot of dedicated men. I never saw one like the Rocket, never saw one born to score goals like he was born to do."

The Kid Who Shot the Rocket

Surely you've seen the photograph. It was taken at Maple Leaf Gardens in the late 1940s and it shows Rocket Richard smashing one of the newly installed panes of Plexiglas with his skate.

A kid photographer snapped the photo of Richard falling to the ice just after his heel shattered the supposedly unbreakable sheet. Standing nearby is Vic Lynn of the Leafs, a look of amazement on his face.

The photo has often been credited to Nat Turofsky, one of two brothers who were the regular photographers at the Gardens.

"But Nat was at the other end of the arena that night and it was some unknown youngster who shot the Rocket," states retired Gardens building superintendent Shanty McKenzie. "The aspiring young photographer kept hounding Nat for a chance to take some photos and Nat finally gave in. But the kid was a bit of a pest so Nat sent him down to the far end. 'Take some shots from down there and stop bugging me,' he said."

The kid wandered down to the corner of the rink just in time to snap one of the most famous photos in hockey history. He shot the Rocket breaking the glass.

Later, nobody could remember the kid's name or recall what happened to him.

But there's an ironic twist to this story. Sitting in behind the glass that night, in the rail seats, with the shattered Plexiglas falling all around them, were the two salesmen who'd sold the Plexiglas sheets to Maple Leaf Gardens.

"It can't be broken," they had boasted when the deal was made.

They didn't know the Rocket.

Rivals Dispute Richard's Toughness

Former Ranger defenceman Ivan Irwin was one of hockey's best fighters in the '50s. On one occasion when the subject of Rocket Richard's fistic abilities was discussed, Irwin said, "Despite the Rocket's reputation as a fighter, I never had much trouble with him. I played against him one night at the Forum, and when he cut in on me I steered him to the outside. Then he swerved to cut inside, brought his stick up and cut me for six stitches over the eye.

"I went off to get stitched up and was back on the ice a few minutes later. Now the Rocket comes in on me again. Once again I steered him outside but he slipped back inside, raised his stick and cut me for six more stitches—about half an inch from the first wound. I was never so mad in my life. Later, in the Ranger zone, I took the feet out from under him and he came at me with his stick. But when he saw that I was ready for him he changed his mind.

"The play went into the Montreal end and I went in there after him. I ran into him and he decided to give me a try. I grabbed him by the scruff of the neck and put him down with his head in between my legs. I dropped to the ice on top of him and he struggled to break loose. But he couldn't move because I was squeezing his ears pretty hard. I said to him, 'You make one more move, Rocket, and I'll break your back.' He said, 'Okay, that's enough.'

"Still, when we went to the penalty box together I made sure Red Storey, the referee, placed a big policeman between us."

Hall-of-Famer Harry Watson was listening and said, "I had a scuffle with him in Chicago. But I never saw the Rocket stand up to anybody. Only once in New York when he stood up to Lou Fontinato. And he didn't stand up too long that time.

"I was playing for Chicago when he and his brother got involved with Al Rollins, our goalie. The Pocket Rocket and Rollins got into a pretty good scrap. Then the Rocket came over and speared Rollins. Really gave him the stick. So I skated over and yanked the stick out of his hands and I threw it away. He went over and got it and came back toward me. I grabbed him and said, 'Give me the stick!' I grabbed it and threw it down and then I grabbed him and threw him up against the glass. I remember he said to me, 'Harry, I don' want you. I don' want you.' That was the end of it. I don't remember that he ever stood up to some of us."

"Guys," I said, "this is the Rocket you're talking about. One of my boy-hood heroes. A flashy, fearless performer who never gave an inch. The guy who kayoed Killer Dill of the Rangers, not once but twice—in the same game. He once flattened Bill Juzda. He had a big reputation as a fighter."

"I think it was more because of the fire in his eyes," said Irwin. "That had a tendency to deter some fellows from fighting him. A much tougher guy was Butch Bouchard. One night Lou Fontinato was roughing up some of the smaller Montreal forwards when Butch, normally a quiet, easygoing fellow, got mad. He took Fontinato by the scruff of the neck, held him up, gave him about five good ones—Pow! Then he pushed him away. Butch never bothered too many of us but we all knew he was the wrong guy to pick on."

Initiation Time

For decades it was a barbaric ritual, indulged in by all NHL clubs. I refer to the annual initiation of rookies, which saw veteran players pin and strip down an unsuspecting first-year player. Wielding razors, they'd proceed to shave the hair from genitals and head, leaving the helpless tenderfoot semi-bald, bruised, and bleeding. Today the ritual is about as common as a straight-bladed stick. On most teams it's been phased out because of severe public criticism of the humiliating practice.

A modern initiation rite involves a team meeting in a posh restaurant, with seven-course meals, fancy wines, and liqueurs—with the rookies footing the bill. The tab often runs into the thousands of dollars. Even so, today's wealthy rookies would rather ante up a few thousand for a meal than suffer the indignity of the old-fashioned initiation.

In 1951, Montreal's John "Goose" McCormack was shaved by his teammates one night and sent to Buffalo of the American League the following day for a week of conditioning. After his first game with the Buffalo farm club, McCormack entered the showers. A teammate glanced down, noticed his hairless condition, and remarked, "Crabs, eh?"

There was the time the team initiated Rocket Richard. The ritual took place on a train rolling toward Montreal after a road game. Richard fought like a tiger and was steaming mad when his initiation was complete. To show his displeasure he grabbed shirts and ties, pajamas and underwear—any clothing his teammates had left in their bunks—and tossed the garb off the train into the night. When the train reached Montreal and the players disembarked, most of them wore their topcoats well buttoned up because they had precious little on underneath, thanks to the Rocket.

Doug Harvey once recalled another incident involving Richard. "We shaved a big cross on Richard's hairy chest one night. It took eight of us to hold him and when he got up there was fire in his eyes. I passed by him a little later and said, 'How's it goin'?' Wham! He smacked me in the face and chipped a couple of teeth. Broke my nose, too. We learned a lesson from that little prank. Never get the Rocket mad. Even if you're his teammate."

Gilles Tremblay told me recently about the initiation of John Ferguson and several other Habs.

"It's hard to believe but one season we had 13 players to initiate. Thirteen in one night. It must be a record. We almost left things too long, you see. Some big boys had joined our club and we kept putting off the ceremony. We'll do it soon or we'll wait until next season, we said. First thing you know there were lots of players who hadn't been initiated and only about eight or ten of us who had. We were almost too scared to do it. We said, 'What if we try to shave these guys and they turn around and shave us? There are enough of them to do it. Then we'll be initiated twice. When the word gets out we'll be the laughing stock of the league.'

"We decided to do it anyway and we picked an all-night-long train ride back from Chicago as the time. We started at about three in the morning and we finished by dawn. We had the most trouble with Fergie, of course, and with Claude LaRose, who hid in the train bathroom. We had to burn papers under the door to smoke him out.

"We were smart to start with Fergie. We all grabbed him and it took all of our strength to hold him down. Geez, did he fight and curse! But when it was over we all patted him on the back and told him what a good fellow he was and that he was on our side now. It didn't seem to matter because he was still hot. Oh, but he was mad! Finally he said, 'Okay, let's go get those other sons of bitches.' And we went after Terry Harper, then Ted Harris and Jimmy Roberts. It was easy with Fergie on our side. Then it was Claude LaRose's turn. He was another strong boy but he had disappeared. But where's he going to hide on a train? We found him locked in the shithouse, sitting in there with 24 beers to last him the rest of the night. By dawn we grew tired of waiting for him to come out so we lit a small fire under the door and smoked him out. The blaze got a little bit out of control but nobody cared. The conductor? What could he do? If he squawked we might have shaved him too.

"The smoke did the job and LaRose barged out of the crapper choking and swearing and full of beer. We stripped him down and did what we had to do. But his was the most expensive initiation. The fire we started did quite a bit of damage and the railroad charged us $400 for repairs."

LaRose has a different recollection of that night. He told me, "I ran like hell for the ladies' washroom and locked myself in, ready to stay the night. I was sitting on the goddam toilet for a couple of hours and I began to get tired. I must have dozed off because suddenly I smelled smoke. Goddam, they'd put a burning rag under the door and I was suffocating. I started choking and yelling and stamping my feet on that rag and finally I got the fire out. It was goddam hot but still I wouldn't budge.

"I waited some more, maybe another hour or two. Then I figure it's safe to come out. I slide the door open and peek out and there's nobody there. I listen and I can hear everybody snoring. So the coast is clear, eh? I tip-toe back to my berth and leap inside. Holy shit! There's Fergie and Talbot waiting for me. They pounce on me and did they give it to me. When they finished I was black all over. They emptied tins of shoe polish on me, stuff they got from Jimmy the porter. What was he gonna say to them? You can't have my shoe polish. Even my ears were plugged full of this shit. Then they shaved me and cut me all over. They woke up the whole train. And they ripped my clothes all to pieces. My pants were cut in half and my coat was torn. When we got to the station in Montreal, I got off the train holding my clothes in front of me. It took me about two weeks to get that stinkin' shoe polish off my body."

In 1964, when the New York Rangers signed Ulf Sterner, one of the first Swedish stars to play in the NHL, he was the recipient of a memorable initiation. One of the roughest of the Rangers grabbed Sterner and hoisted him in the air, breaking two of his ribs.

Curry's Hat Trick Saved His Job

Floyd "Busher" Curry will never forget the night he produced the only hat trick of his ten-year NHL career. His timing couldn't have been better.

In 1951, visiting the Forum as one stop on her royal tour of Canada was Princess Elizabeth. The Forum faithful were abuzz with excitement as the Princess took her place in the arena.

On the ice, Floyd Curry pumped himself up for the game, not only because the future Queen would be watching but because a strange premonition came to him. In the days leading up to the game, Curry had the uneasy feeling that another so-so performance would find him on a train to the minor leagues. The thought was a sobering one.

Throughout the match he sparkled like glass in a chandelier. And at the end of the evening he was the leading marksman on both sides with a three-goal "hat trick." After the match, while hockey men at the side of the Princess explained the term "hat trick," a beaming Curry sat in the

Montreal dressing room surrounded by reporters. They all wanted to know how it felt to collect three goals on such a special night. Curry gave them a memorable comment.

"Aw, it was nuthin'," he explained. "You fellows know I always play well in front of royalty."

Curry's goal-scoring spree kept him with the Habs, and it wasn't until he was long retired from the game that general manager Frank Selke admitted that Curry's premonition had been an accurate one. The Habs were thinking of sending him to the minors—until he entertained a visiting princess with three flashy goals. It turned out to be the only hat trick of his NHL career.

"Think of how many I might have had," he once said, "if the Princess had become a season ticket holder."

Beliveau's First Trick

On December 15, 1952, the daily newspapers in Montreal gave full attention to a young phenom from Quebec City, a softspoken centreman who, in a smashing performance the night before, had rapped in three goals for the Canadiens.

It was a brilliant game for Kid Beliveau. Here's how the game was described in one Montreal paper.

Montreal, Dec. 19—As the immortal Maurice the Rocket Richard sat virtually alone unlacing his skates in the Montreal Canadien dressing room last night, photographers and well-wishers crowded around Jean Marc Beliveau, a gangling kid with a winning smile and a dynamite-laden stick.

Richard didn't mind the three goals Kid Beliveau scored to lead the Habs to their 6–2 win over New York. But the cheers the crowd showered on the youngster fresh from the senior ranks were the cheers Montrealers usually reserved for the Rocket.

The customers used to cover the ice with programs, rubbers and cop-pers at Richard's every goal. Last night, the old pro was just another figure as youth busted out all over.

EXPLOSION.

The fans raised the roof from the time Beliveau rapped in the Rocket's rebound for his first goal until he faked Ranger defenseman Steve Kraftcheck practically out of his skates to complete a sensational debut.

The kid admitted the night provided "the greatest thrill" of his hockey career. "Everything was right," he said. "I was getting all the breaks."

Beliveau is certain to move up to the Canadiens next year, and prob-ably will still make the $15,000 he receives in Quebec City.

Coach Dick Irvin wished he didn't have to wait so long. "He's a great hockey player," Irvin said. "We could certainly use him this year."

If Kid Beliveau decides to forsake his reputation as the highest paid ama-teur in the country, it is sure to bring about a complete split in the affection of Canadiens' fans, and it's doubtful if the split would go against Beliveau.

Old pro Richard, at 31 and in his 12th season may have a few more years left. But the writing was on the wall last night. His place at the top of the fans' popularity parade had been taken over, at least temporarily, by Kid Beliveau.

OOPS!

"What do you think of your new linemate?" a reporter asked Richard.

"That's one hell of a question to ask me," he replied.

He seemed to be remembering the just-completed game in which he set up all three goals for a kid named Beliveau and heard only the echo of a cheering crowd.

Beliveau had played in two previous games for the Habs, in 1950–51, and was named the game's first star in his debut despite going scoreless. In 1952–53 he scored five times in the three games he played.

As a junior player in 1951, I was given the difficult (impossible?) assignment of checking Beliveau in an Eastern Canada junior playoff series. I recall being intimidated by his huge reputation—and his huge size—on the opening faceoff. He was a giant, the biggest centreman I'd ever seen. When I see him today I wonder if he's shrunk over the years, for he looks far less massive. There are dozens of NHLers who are bigger. But how he could play the game! He sifted through us like we were a bunch of pee wees.

In Quebec City, before one of our games, his grateful fans presented him with a new car. I recall that it was a Nash. I doubt that anyone on our club owned a car—certainly not a new one.

Former Leaf captain Darryl Sittler once told me he too experienced a sense of awe the first time he faced off against Beliveau. "I remember the strange feeling that came over me when I looked up at him," Sittler recalled. "He was right in front of me, just inches away. I was about to battle for the puck with the great Beliveau, my boyhood hero.

"Years later," Sittler added, "after Jean had ended his brilliant career, I was going through some difficult times in Toronto when I received the nicest letter from him, offering me words of encouragement. I'll never forget it. His words really moved me."

The Reluctant Goalie

Before his death in 1972, Bill Durnan, Hall-of-Fame goaltender, enjoyed kibitzing with his pals around the bar of the Toronto Press Club. I would see him there, in the company of Ted Reeve, the renowned sports columnist, or Tommy "Windy" O'Neil, the Leaf forward turned lawyer.

When I joined the group from time to time, I always hoped Durnan would talk about his glory days with the Montreal Canadiens. But he seldom did. He much preferred others to carry the conversational ball.

He did tell me one humorous story. It was about a minor-league goalie named Alex Woods. "He did something in a game one night I always longed to do in Montreal. But with Dick Irvin as my coach I wouldn't dare. Woods's team was losing by a big score, 8–0 or 9–1, something like that, when an opposing player got a breakaway. Just as the player was about to shoot on goal, Woods stepped out of the net, waved his stick at the empty cage, and said 'Be my guest.'"

A major reason Durnan was never able to emulate Woods was that, in a Canadiens uniform, Durnan seldom if ever allowed a rival team to pile up a score. There is no question: in a short career, he established himself as one of the greatest goalies of all time.

And yet he was a most reluctant recruit to big-league hockey, failing to make his debut in the NHL until he was 27 years old. It wasn't as though he was suddenly transformed from a mediocre goalie into a great one overnight. He'd always had outstanding ability, right from the time he was a teenager playing in his native Toronto. Certainly the Leafs showed interest in him and offered him a position on one of their sponsored junior teams. But Durnan opted to play in Sudbury, where he took a job and starred for the Sudbury Wolves, leading them to the Memorial Cup.

The Leafs came after him again, and offered him a pro contract. But he twisted a knee, and when the Leafs saw him walking with a limp, they withdrew their offer. After all, there were plenty of promising goaltenders around in those days and only a handful were needed to stock all the teams in the NHL.

Durnan shrugged off the slight and turned to his other love—softball. He was a superb pitcher and in 1936 he guided a Kirkland Lake team to the Ontario championship. Later Kirkland Lake formed a senior amateur hockey team, the Blue Devils. Durnan, who'd all but retired from hockey, was invited to play for them. He led the Devils to the Allan Cup title in 1940.

The following year he moved to Montreal to play for the Montreal Royals, a Canadiens farm team. He had a good job and playing for the Royals was fun. He had no ambition to join the Habs. Paul Bibeault (the only Hab ever to wear a zero on his back) was the Montreal netminder. Durnan was impressed with Bibeault's skills and had no desire to replace him.

Then came news that Bibeault had enlisted in the Canadian army. It was 1943 and Tommy Gorman, Montreal's general manager, approached Durnan and offered him the job as Bibeault's replacement. Durnan demurred. He told Gorman it would take a lot of money to pull him away from his current position. The two men negotiated back and forth throughout the ten-day training camp, which was held at night to accommodate the war workers on the club. The 1943–44 NHL season was about to begin and Gorman was on the spot. He would be forced to employ a 17-year-old kid named Gerry McNeil if Durnan didn't sign.

When Gorman upped the ante only minutes before the opening faceoff, Durnan signed the contract, donned his goal pads, and sparkled in his NHL debut, a 2–2 tie with the Boston Bruins. He continued to shine throughout the first month of play and accumulated 14 straight wins before suffering his first defeat. By January 10, he had won 20 and lost only two. The Habs won 38 of 50 games that year, tied seven, and lost only five. The team finished 25 points ahead of second-place Detroit and Durnan allowed only 109 goals, 65 fewer than his nearest rival. Montrealers howled in anger when Toronto's Gus Bodnar (with a rookie record of 62 points) was awarded the Calder Trophy as Rookie of the Year. They felt the honour belonged to Durnan.

There was some compensation. Durnan captured the Vezina Trophy with a 2.18 goals-against average. He was even stingier in the playoffs, allowing 14 goals in nine games (a 1.53 average) as the Habs swept to the Stanley Cup, whipping Toronto in the semis and Chicago in the finals. The Canadiens' only postseason loss was to Toronto in the opening game of the first round.

Former referee Bill Chadwick once said, "Durnan was the finest goal-tender I ever saw, but in the playoffs, Turk Broda of Toronto was his equal. Durnan was ambidextrous. He'd come out there wearing conventional gloves on both hands and he could switch his stick from hand to hand, depending on which side of the ice the play was coming from. And he was a terrific puckhandler. He was one of the first to develop that ability, and although he couldn't handle the puck as well as, say, Jacques Plante, he still helped himself a great deal with that special ability."

Fake! Fake! Fake!

In the spring of 1944, the Montreal Canadiens were on the verge of winning the Stanley Cup. With rookie goaltender Bill Durnan enjoying a most remarkable NHL debut, and Rocket Richard at his peak, the Habs had swept past Toronto in five games and were undefeated after three matches with Chicago in the final series. For some reason, the first and fourth games of the final series were played in Montreal, the second and third in Chicago. Montreal took the opener 5–1 and two nights later Rocket Richard's three goals gave the Habs a 3–1 victory in Chicago. The third game at the Chicago Stadium was closer: a 3–2 victory for Montreal.

Back at the Forum for game four, a huge crowd turned out to see the Habs win the Cup on home ice. But the Blackhawks silenced the crowd by racing out to a 4–1 lead. At the start of the third period, the crowd turned ugly. Many felt the Habs were deliberately losing the game to extend the series. "Fake! Fake! Fake!" they roared at the Habs before the puck was dropped to begin the period. Their anger was like a slap in the face to the vaunted Punch Line, which had been held to a single goal. Richard, Blake, and Lach seethed with indignation. To accuse them of not trying was unthinkable. If the fans wanted a comeback—and a Cup win—that's what they'd get. Bang,

bang, bang! The Canadiens lit the red light three times. Richard's second goal of the game tied the score. He looked up as if to say "Take that!" Toe Blake's marker midway through the first overtime won the game. Fan anger had long since dissipated. It had turned to joy, to worship, to elation. The Habs had captured the Stanley Cup for the first time in 13 years.

Coach Dick Irvin would say of the jeering mob, "There are always people who think everything is fixed and I suspect they must be shady themselves. The chanting that night made my players see red. Why, they tied the score within ten minutes after hearing those taunts and Toe Blake almost tore off the back of the net with his overtime counter."

Doug Harvey: Marching to a Different Drum

When he died of cirrhosis of the liver on that cold December day in 1989, hockey men were quick to react to the passing of Doug Harvey. "When I joined Montreal," said Jean Beliveau, "he was the best defenceman I'd ever seen."

"I feel very sad," said Maurice Richard, "We had a lot of fun together. Doug was great, always willing to help."

"Harvey was the best defenceman of our day," added former Leaf captain George Armstrong. "Playing against him was like playing against Wayne Gretzky or Bobby Orr. Those kind of players always find a way to beat you."

Howie Meeker, another ex-Leaf who played against Harvey for several seasons, recalled the defenceman's ability to control a game. "The tough son of a gun always came out of nowhere to become the biggest thorn in our side. He was a '50s Bobby Orr, only a shade slower. He was a Mack truck for Montreal, always controlling the pace of the game. You knew what he was doing, you could see him do it. But you couldn't do much about it."

Doug Harvey had an unselfish nature and a flair for the dramatic. Late in the season in 1948, teammate Elmer Lach needed one point to win the

NHL scoring title. Harvey made a grand rush up the ice late in the final game, pulled the opposing goalie, and flipped the puck across to Lach, who slapped it in.

When Harvey broke in with Montreal in 1947–48, fans would have scoffed it they'd been told this lackadaisical rookie would lead the Canadiens to six Stanley Cups. And capture seven Norris Trophies as the NHL's top defenceman. Or play 20 NHL seasons and be named a first-team All-Star ten times.

They didn't see his talent at first, only his lack of it. They booed him when they first saw him play. He looked so nonchalant, so hesitant, even careless with the puck in the Montreal zone. Initially his style drove coach Dick Irvin to distraction. And yet, despite his imperfections, he never seemed to cough up the puck or make a big mistake. And he controlled the tempo of the game like no other player in history. In time, everyone relaxed. They began to appreciate his novel approach and the plaudits began to pour in. He shrugged them off. Despite all the team and personal accomplishments that followed, triumphs that gave Montreal fans so much joy and happiness, Harvey himself was seldom happy. He was a troubled man.

He was known as a drinking man who cursed and raged against the hockey establishment. "I didn't drink," he'd protest, "unless I was real thirsty." He was an angry man who snarled at the mention of hockey pioneers like Frank Selke and Conn Smythe. For many years Smythe managed to keep Busher Jackson, a noted alcoholic, out of the Hockey Hall of Fame. "What the bleep did Smythe know about beating them in the alley?" Harvey asked. "His son [Stafford] was even worse."

When Harvey was ignored by the Hall of Fame selection committee in 1972, the year they bent the rules to usher in Gordie Howe and Jean Beliveau, he blamed Selke. "They don't want me in there because I've been known to hoist a few," he said. "At least I don't sneak around the corner to drink, like some guys. And they've never forgiven Ted Lindsay and myself for helping form the NHL Players' Association. We were blackballed when we did that."

The Hall of Fame welcomed Harvey the following year but, still angry, he ignored the honour. "I'll be out fishing that day," he said, and he kept his word, failing to show for the once-in-a-lifetime ceremony.

In the mid-'80s the Canadiens finally got around to retiring Harvey's famous jersey number 2. Camil DesRoches, a public-relations fixture at the Forum for decades, arranged a dinner for Doug, his family, and 35 of his friends. "It was a joyous occasion," recalled DesRoches, who, as the youngest of 19 in his own family, knew about such things. "The following night Doug's sweater was retired before the Hartford game. The ceremony was on national TV."

Aside from Harvey's number 2, the Canadiens have retired number 4 (Beliveau), number 7 (Morenz), number 9 (Maurice Richard), number 10 (Guy Lafleur), and number 16 (Henri Richard and Elmer Lach).

I saw Harvey perform on the baseball diamond long before I saw him on skates. It was in Ottawa in the late '40s. I remember him as an outstanding ballplayer. He batted .351 with the Class C Ottawa Nationals one season. I had heard he was headed for a major-league career with the Boston Braves, who sought his services. But Harvey's first love was always hockey, although he was also a brilliant football player who just missed playing on a Grey Cup winner in 1944. That was the season he quit football to join the Royal Canadian Navy. "Sorry boys, but I have to go to war," he explained. It was said he could punt a football 65 yards. In the navy he turned to boxing and won the Canadian Navy heavyweight boxing championship.

Harvey joined the Canadiens in 1947–48 and quickly proved himself the equal of any of hockey's greatest defenders. But marching to his own drum did not sit well with some of the executives around him. When the Canadiens required a captain to replace Butch Bouchard in 1956, the players were quietly urged to vote for Maurice Richard and ignore Harvey, despite his obvious leadership qualities.

When things were not going well, it was Harvey who often called a team meeting to straighten things out. The other Habs looked up to him. But after helping the Canadiens win five consecutive Cups (1956–60), he was traded to New York in 1961, even though he was a first-team All-Star and holder of the Norris Trophy.

"I would have been traded earlier," he once said. "But we kept winning all those Cups. Selke knew if he traded me then the fans would have rioted."

With the Rangers, as player-coach, Harvey led the team into the play-offs for the first time in years (1958), but he gave up the coaching job after one season. "I liked the playing part best," he said. "You know, being with the boys, tossing back a few after the game. Having fun. I never really liked coaching that much."

He played briefly with the Red Wings in 1966–67 and joined the St. Louis Blues for the playoffs in 1968. His final season was in 1968–69, when he gave the Blues the best a 45-year-old could offer.

When the WHA needed experienced hockey men in the '70s, Harvey joined the Houston Aeros as assistant manager to Bill Dineen. He is credited with suggesting that the Aeros sign two underage players, Mark and Marty Howe, to pro contracts. They signed, and their old man was so excited about the deal that he decided to come out of retirement and play for the Aeros too.

Knock, Knock. Who's There?

When Andra McLaughlin, the professional figure skater, was dating Red Kelly, hockey star with Detroit, her family frowned on the idea of marriage. So her father sent her off to South Africa for a few weeks. There she discovered a huge ice-skating rink that was used for hockey by a number of

Canadians living there. Andra recalls that the players had only 12 uniforms. A dozen players would suit up, play until they grew tired, then strip down and another dozen players would don the same sweaty outfits. But Andra recalls an even bigger surprise. On the wall at the end of the arena, someone had hung a huge portrait of Rocket Richard.

Later, when Andra joined a touring ice show and shared a dressing room with Barbara Ann Scott, Canadian Olympic champion in 1948, from time to time there would be a knock on their dressing-room door.

"Who is it?" Andra would call out.

"It's the world's greatest hockey player," was the answer.

When Andra threw open the door, Red Kelly would be standing there. One night the skaters were performing at the Montreal Forum. Before the show there was a knock on the door.

"Who is it?" Andra called out.

"It's the world's greatest hockey player," was the muffled response.

Andra was surprised. She knew Red was on the road with the Red Wings. How was it possible he was in Montreal?

When she threw open the door, standing there, a big grin on his face was...Rocket Richard!

The little prank had been engineered by Camil DesRoches of the Canadiens' publicity department.

Selke and Pollock: Two of a Kind

Frank Selke was born in a town that no longer exists, Berlin, Ontario, in 1893. Berlin became Kitchener, and residents of that German community proudly claim Boston's Kraut Line as three native sons who excelled on ice. The Poles in town claim that Selke's hockey contributions, as a non-skater, were just as immense.

Too small to make a career of the game as a player, as a teenager Selke showed uncanny ability to organize teams. His talents soon caught the eye of Conn Smythe, who was scrambling up the hockey ladder in Toronto. They made a formidable team in the late '20s, when Smythe decided to build a new home for his Maple Leafs, an ice palace called Maple Leaf Gardens.

It was Selke, an electrician by trade, who convinced members of the trade unions to take back Gardens stock in lieu of cash when construction was underway. He even mortgaged his new home to buy stock—and never regretted it.

For the next decade and a half, the famous duo of Smythe and Selke helped make the Leafs and the Gardens world-famous and a huge financial success. During the war years it was Selke who directed operations at the Gardens while Smythe was serving overseas. When Smythe returned, he complained about some of Selke's decisions, especially a deal Selke made with Montreal, when he "stole" Ted Kennedy away from the Habs in return for Frankie Eddolls, a Smythe favourite. Selke resented the criticism and soon the friction between them became intolerable.

He left Smythe and the Leafs in the spring of 1946, thinking he might wind up in Cincinnati to head up a new arena project. But William Northey, managing director of the Montreal Canadiens, offered him a position as manager of the Forum and the Canadiens Hockey Club. It was a challenge that Selke couldn't refuse.

Arriving in Montreal, he immediately unveiled plans to revitalize the Montreal farm system. It wasn't long before amateur teams across Canada, supervised by astute hockey men like Sam Pollock and Ken Reardon, were producing talented players for the Habs. Selke then set about refurbishing the antiquated Forum. He raised the roof and installed 3,500 more seats, adding to the former capacity of 9,600. He hired a team of plumbers and painters (the old seats were all brown in colour), and the spruced-up Forum was transformed from an ugly duckling into a showcase for the sport.

It was Selke who recognized the coaching genius of first Dick Irvin and later Toe Blake. When Blake replaced Irvin in 1955, the Habs rattled off a record five Stanley Cup wins in a row.

Between 1946, when Selke took command, and 1964, when he retired, the Canadiens missed the playoffs only once, in 1948. During his term they won six Stanley Cups. In retirement he was made an honorary governor of the NHL for life. One of his proudest accomplishments was helping to establish the Hockey Hall of Fame in Toronto. In 1960 he became an honoured member, having served hockey faithfully for over half a century.

Sam Pollock, like Selke, discovered early in life that he had a flair for organizing teams, even the teams he played on. Born in Montreal's suburb of Notre Dame de Grace, he grew up to become a loyal railway worker, with a reputation for knowing at all times where all the boxcars were located.

He soon found that keeping track of hockey players was much more fun. He started in the Montreal organization as a gofer, a lowly errand boy, then went on to scout, sign, and manage dozens of minor-leaguers who went on to stardom with the parent club. When Selke retired in 1964, Pollock was a ready and willing replacement.

He quickly established himself as a master of the trade, a shrewd dispenser of surplus talent in return for draft choices (which is how Montreal acquired Guy Lafleur). He was equally crafty at the draft table. In 1973, he swapped draft positions with the Atlanta Flames (who wanted Tom Lysiak) and the St. Louis Blues (who coveted John Davidson). Atlanta and St. Louis got their men while Sam plucked Bob Gainey out of the same draft when his turn came. Take a bow, Sam. What's more, as part of the deal, Pollock received two first-round choices from Atlanta and St. Louis for the following year, 1974. One year later, using those picks, he added Doug Risebrough and Rick Chartraw to the Habs stable.

Over the years he earned the nickname "Sad Sam" for his dour, worried expression. He had little to worry about. His Canadiens won nine Stanley Cups between 1964 and 1978. That year, at age 53, he retired from the Habs' front office to enter the world of business. He was persuaded to retain a hockey connection as director of player development with Hockey Canada. He was inducted into the Hockey Hall of Fame in 1978—the youngest man ever named to the builders' category.

Chapter 5
THE TOE BLAKE ERA

Toe's First Coaching Triumph

When hockey fans recall the 1950s, they think of five consecutive Stanley Cups won by the Canadiens. Yet it was an era when the Detroit Red Wings might easily have equalled or surpassed that record—with a break or two. Detroit finished atop the regular-season standings seven straight times from 1949 to 1955. Twice they finished with 44 victories and over 100 points to rewrite the NHL record book. Twice Gordie Howe and Ted Lindsay finished one-two in the individual scoring race. But instead of seven Stanley Cups, they wound up with only four. And most Montrealers felt Detroit's Cup win in 1955 was tainted; it was the year the Rocket was suspended.

Rookie coach Toe Blake nervously took his place behind the Montreal bench for the 1955–56 season. He was filling Dick Irvin's shoes and he knew it would take some time to break them in. But he needn't have worried about blisters or bunions, for he was blessed with a "dream team," one that would dominate the NHL like no team before it. Blake's men racked up a record 45 wins and 100 points, and finished an awesome 24 points in front of second-place Detroit.

Jean Beliveau had developed into hockey's best centreman, firing 47 goals and adding 41 assists to win the scoring title and the Art Ross Trophy. He was also named league MVP. Jacques Plante captured the Vezina as the stingiest netminder. His goals-against average was a niggardly 1.86. Bert Olmstead set a record for assists by a left winger with 56. Four Habs—Plante, Beliveau, Doug Harvey, and Maurice Richard—were named to the first All-Star team. Tom Johnson and Bert Olmstead captured berths on the second team.

In the playoffs, the Habs lost just two of ten games, eliminating first the Rangers and then the Red Wings, both by margins of four games to one.

Blake often said that his 1956 Canadiens gave him a great deal of satisfaction. "First they finished in first place over Detroit during the regular schedule. Then they knocked the Red Wings out in the finals. Remember, the Red Wings had been the dominant team in hockey for years. And it was a big thrill to win the Cup in my first season as coach."

Irvin's shoes had lost some of their squeak by then. Four years later, when the Habs had added four more Cup wins, Irvin's brogans were long forgotten and Blake's smooth footwork behind the bench was the talk of hockey as he put the boots to all who challenged his mighty machine.

Although he played on three Stanley Cup winners and starred on Montreal's famous Punch Line, Hector "Toe" Blake gained true hockey fame as one of hockey's most successful coaches. He guided hockey's most prominent franchise to eight Stanley Cups in 13 seasons.

As a player, he won his first Stanley Cup as a member of the Montreal Maroons in 1934–35, although he was mostly a bench sitter as a rookie, suiting up for one playoff game. He was traded to the Canadiens and in 1938–39 won the Art Ross Trophy as the NHL's leading scorer with 24 goals and 23 assists. In 1945–46 he served just one minor penalty and won the Lady Byng Trophy as the league's most gentlemanly player. He scored 235 goals and 527 points in his NHL career, which ended when he broke his leg on January 10, 1948.

Bonin the Bear Wrestler

I cozied up to Marcel Bonin at the Montreal Forum one morning while the Habs were at practice and he told me some fascinating things about his life, both in and out of hockey.

"Back in '51 I was playing for the Quebec Aces after my junior days with Three Rivers. One night in Quebec we played the Detroit Red Wings in an exhibition game. Punch Imlach was my coach and he came to me and said, 'Marcel, you be careful out there tonight. If you get in a fight with Ted Lindsay, he's one tough son of a bitch and he never drops his stick. Remember that.'

"So I remembered that, and Punch was right. I ran into Lindsay and he snarled something at me, so I threw off a glove and knocked him cold with one punch. Sure enough, even out cold, he was still hanging onto his stick.

"It wasn't long before I was Lindsay's teammate in Detroit. That's where I began my NHL career. You know, I never had to take the plane before. So I take the plane to Detroit. And I never spoke any English. I sign a contract with Mr. Adams and the next day they put me on another plane and send me to St. Louis. That's where I learn how to play pro hockey.

"Finally I get called up to Detroit and my first NHL game was against the Canadiens at the Forum. I remember it was the same game that Glenn Hall got started in the NHL because Terry Sawchuk was hurt.

"By 1957 I was with the Canadiens and was a member of one of the greatest teams of all time. I helped them win three straight Stanley Cups— the final three years of their five-year reign.

"The best memory I have of hockey is the friendship of my teammates. They were all just like brothers. Because at first I didn't speak English I wanted them to pay attention to me. So I'd put a needle through my arm or I'd eat some glass—things like that—just to make them laugh. And they liked that. But they never made fun of me. They laughed with me. In Montreal I used to be all the time with Claude Provost, Jean Guy Talbot, and Maurice Richard. And my buddy on the road was Dickie Moore. Everybody remembers Dickie. He was a winner, a great two-way player. He liked to play jokes on people too. One day Tom Johnson got a new car and parked it near the Forum. When he came out to get it, the whole front seat was filled with big chunks of snow and ice from the street. Guess who did that?

"And the Rocket, ha ha. He was a big leader. He hated to lose, I mean hated it—even in the practice. So he gave us the spirit and when I was a kid he was my idol. Before that my idol was Howie Morenz but not like the Rocket. I was just a kid then. And when Howie Morenz died—it was in 1937, I think—they put his death in all the papers. My father was very sad. He was a bus driver in Montreal and he brought me to see Morenz play one night. Morenz had been traded away to Chicago and when he came back to the Forum my father took me to see him play—only once.

"Many of the best players in the world were my teammates. Jacques Plante was one of the best goalies who ever played. Oh, I remember when Toe Blake didn't want him to wear that mask. Every team had only one goalie in those days and none of them wore a mask.

"Jean Beliveau has been a good friend. He's a good businessman too. I played with him in Quebec for two years and in Montreal for five. A real gentleman. I told him not long ago to stay home and enjoy the rest of his life. Don't work so hard. Me, I do nothing. I was sick a few years ago and the doctor said, 'Marcel, you better stay home.' So I stayed home and I bought some books, beautiful books. I never ever read before. Never went to school. Now I love those books, especially the history books. It's too bad I missed all those years by not reading.

"In the books, I discovered that many great men came from Quebec. Mr. Cadillac went to Detroit. La Verendrye went to the Rockies. They all started from right here. That is very interesting to read about that.

"I know, I know, you want to hear about the bear wrestling. Well, it happened like this. When Joe Louis, the heavyweight boxing champion, retired, he went with the circus because even after all those big fights he had no money. He was a kind of referee, a guy who talked people into wrestling this bear. He said he'd give a thousand dollars to anyone who could put the bear down. And lots of people came and tried.

"Well, I was about 16 and I said, 'I'm gonna go.' So I left my home in Joliette and I wrestled that bear. But he was big and strong and I couldn't put him down.

"But I wouldn't give up. I went to Three Rivers and a lot of other places and I wrestled that bear lots of times. After a while I got to be buddies with that bear. He was a big brown bear with a muzzle and no claws. In lots of towns in Quebec, people still remember Marcel the bear wrestler.

"When I got into hockey with Detroit, Marcel Pronovost told a lot of people about my bear-wrestling and they made a big story about it."

Boom Boom Goes for the Record

Boom Boom Geoffrion's NHL career almost came to an end during a routine practice session at the Montreal Forum. It happened on January 28, 1958. Geoffrion collided with a teammate and immediately fell to the ice, doubled over in pain. Before he lapsed into unconsciousness, he told his mates, "Somebody get me a priest."

The problem was a ruptured intestine. Geoffrion was rushed to a nearby hospital, where he underwent emergency surgery. There were reports that his pulse had stopped for at least 15 seconds. He was a very sick individual.

During his recovery Geoffrion's wife, Marlene (daughter of Howie Morenz), pleaded with her husband to give up the game.

"My father died from hockey," she told him. "I don't want to lose you too."

Boom Boom said he would think about it. But as he regained his strength, he knew it was far too early to quit. He was, after all, a key performer on what many were calling "the greatest hockey team ever assembled," a club that had won two straight Stanley Cups and was almost halfway to a record five.

What's more, Geoffrion had a couple of personal goals he wanted to achieve before hanging up his skates. First, he had a burning desire to surpass the number of career goals his illustrious father-in-law had scored: 270. And he wanted a crack at Rocket Richard's record of 50 goals in 50 games, a mark established back in 1944–45.

His fans had always predicted huge things in hockey for Geoffrion, but he always seemed to fall short of their expectations. There was still much for him to achieve.

Injuries had been a major problem. Aside from the ruptured intestine, they included two shoulder separations, three broken ribs, a fractured wrist, four broken noses, a broken ankle, and a broken toe. In his only injury-free season—1954–55, the year he was booed for winning the Art Ross Trophy when he edged suspended teammate Rocket Richard—he finished with 38 goals and 75 points. He would set no records in 1957–58, for the intestinal operation kept him out of the lineup for 28 games.

When the 1960–61 season opened, Geoffrion was in good health and cautiously optimistic about his prospects for the next six months. By then, at age 29, he had 254 goals and needed 16 more to tie the mark of Morenz. By early December he had potted 15.

On December 7, 1960, the Habs were in Toronto for a game with the Leafs. When Boom Boom called home that day, his son Danny made him promise to score two goals "so that you'll have more than Mama's daddy had."

That night, at 9:13 of the first period, Jean Beliveau fed Boom Boom a pass and he slammed the puck past goalie Johnny Bower for his 270th goal.

He had tied Morenz!

Beliveau led another rush a few minutes later, and pushed the puck ahead to Geoffrion, who slapped one from inside the Leaf blue line. The red light flashed, signalling goal number 271. At that moment Geoffrion became the fifth-highest scorer in NHL history, behind Rocket Richard, Gordie Howe, Ted Lindsay, and Nels Stewart.

With 17 goals, Geoffrion began to focus on a 50-goal season. But most of the goal-scoring excitement that season was created by a Toronto left winger, a lanky 23-year-old named Frank Mahovlich. Mahovlich had 24 goals, and by mid-January he was ahead of Geoffrion 37 to 27.

That's when another injury—a strained knee—sent Geoffrion to the sidelines for several days and cost him six games. With 15 games left to play, Mahovlich had 43 goals, Geoffrion 32.

Would the Big M surpass the Rocket? That was the question everyone was asking. Geoffrion? Nobody even considered him a threat.

Perhaps it made Boom Boom mad. Perhaps he knew it would be his last chance to see his name in the record book, alongside his boyhood idol and teammate, the mighty Rocket.

Something inspired him to play even better. In the next two games he scored five times. Then he scored three more goals. When he hit 40 goals (Mahovlich had 45) your author was a late-night sports reporter on CFCF-TV in Montreal. I made a bold prediction one night—who knows why?—and called for Geoffrion to score ten goals in the next ten games to tie the Rocket. I can't recall what I predicted for Mahovlich, or if I even mentioned him. Perhaps I assumed the Big M would tie the mark too, or break it.

Anyway, Geoffrion made me look like a true psychic as he embarked on a memorable scoring spree. He scored three goals in one game and two in another. He tied Mahovlich, then passed him. With three games left to play, it was Geoffrion 49, Mahovlich 47.

The next game for Geoffrion was at the Forum against Mahovlich and the Leafs. It was March 16, 1961.

I sent a cameraman to the Forum and ordered him to follow Geoffrion's every move from the moment he stepped on the ice. I shuddered to think that Boom Boom would score and we wouldn't have the highlights for our late-night news, weather, and sports package.

The Leafs' Bert Olmstead shadowed Geoffrion that night and stuck to him like a wet shirt, bottling him up through two periods of play. With ten minutes left in the game and the Canadiens leading 4–2, Geoffrion had a marvellous chance. He pulled goalie Cesare Maniago out of position, shot—and hit the post!

High in the crowd, rubbing shoulders with the fans, my conscientious cameraman captured the action on film. But when Boom Boom hit the post, a fan jumped up in front of his camera and, waving his arms in excitement, struck the cameraman on the hand.

The cameraman howled in pain and stopped filming for a few seconds. He cursed the fan, shook his injured hand in the air, blew on it, and prepared to resume filming.

You guessed it. At that precise moment, Geoffrion scored!

Beliveau had won a faceoff and whipped the puck to Gilles Tremblay, who swiftly relayed it to Geoffrion. Instinctively he fired the rubber past Maniago and the Forum rocked. Red Fisher said it was "like Christmas and New Year's Eve and everybody's birthday. The fans rose to their feet with a tremendous roar. A piercing whistle sang across the Forum and from the seats came the rubbers, the programs and the hats…" On the ice, Geoffrion was locked in the arms of Beliveau and in seconds the two were buried under a sea of red, white, and blue jerseys.

Back at the TV station, I whooped for joy. Geoffrion had tied the record and my bold prediction had come true. In a few minutes the cameraman would arrive with the precious film of the historic moment in hand.

I greeted him when he burst through the door.

"Have you got the film?"

"Sure do. Got it right here."

"Great! Let's get it edited and on the air."

"There's just one problem."

"What's that?"

"I missed the damn goal. You see, this idiot in front of me jumped up and hit my hand. That's when Boom Boom scored. Sorry about that." His face brightened. "But I've got lots of footage of guys congratulating Geoffrion. And a good shot of him almost scoring, only he hit the post. We could use that sequence and viewers might think it was his 50th."

I had a sudden urge to throttle the man. How could he shoot hundreds of feet of costly film and miss Geoffrion's historic marker?

But he did. He had.

If you'd seen our coverage that night you would have been impressed. Several shots of Geoffrion skating and shooting. A great shot of him hitting the goal post. And shots of people congratulating him and falling on top of him. As for the goal itself, you probably thought you blinked and missed it. That's what we hoped, anyway.

Boom Boom Shakes Cast

There was a playoff series between Montreal and Chicago in the spring of 1961. Boom Boom Geoffrion, one of Montreal's top snipers, was on the limp, his knee encased in a plaster cast because of a late-season injury.

"I thought I might be able to play," recalls Boom Boom. "But the doctor said no. Leave the cast on for another couple of weeks.

"I went to Chicago anyway—to be with the team. On the train, I decided to ignore the doctor and get rid of the damn cast. I went in the ladies' room with Doug Harvey and I told him, 'Help me get rid of this cast.' He said, 'Okay,' and he tried removing it with a straight razor. Well, that didn't work so he found some scissors and started cutting away at it. Took him three hours to pop it loose.

"The knee was very wobbly but I told Toe Blake I could play and I dressed for the game. They froze the knee and I wasn't on the ice five minutes when Bobby Hull ran into me and put me out of the game. They put another cast on the knee and it took all summer to heal. When I look back, I think it was a stupid, smart-aleck thing to do, taking that cast off, but sometimes hockey players will do anything to get back on the ice."

Five in a Row Is Fantastic

The 1959–60 season was another banner year for the Canadiens. The regular schedule ended with Montreal in first place with 40 wins and 92 points— 13 points more than second-place Toronto. The other two clubs to fight their way into the postseason, third-place Chicago and fourth-place Detroit, had played under-.500 hockey and managed only 69 and 67 points respectively.

Now the Habs set out to capture an unprecedented fifth consecutive Stanley Cup. The roster was basically the same as the one that had started the dynasty back in 1955–56. Still with the club were future Hall-of-Famers Jacques Plante, Doug Harvey, Tom Johnson, Maurice and Henri Richard, Boom Boom Geoffrion, Dickie Moore, and Jean Beliveau.

But many of these heroes were getting on in years. Injuries were beginning to take their toll. Other teams were getting stronger. The Habs would face Chicago in the first round and there were fears that two rising stars, Bobby Hull and Stan Mikita, combined with Glenn Hall's masterful goaltending, would derail the Canadiens.

But the Habs handled the Hawks easily, sweeping the series in four straight games and outscoring their opponents 14–6.

Now Toe Blake's men braced themselves for the finals against Toronto. New coach Punch Imlach was attempting to build a dynasty of his own with the Leafs, a team that gained strength and confidence as the season wound down.

Imlach showed up for the first game at the Forum with several four-leaf clovers pinned to his clothes. But the foliage brought him no luck once the puck was dropped. The Habs banged in three goals before the 12-minute mark and coasted to a 4–2 victory.

In game two Moore and Beliveau scored in the first six minutes of play. The Leafs got one back but they couldn't stick the puck past Plante for the equalizer. Montreal 2, Toronto 1. Game three in Toronto resulted in an easy 5–2 win for Montreal, highlighted by the goaltending wizardry of Jacques Plante and Rocket Richard's first goal of the 1960 playoffs. It was Richard's 82nd playoff goal, the most in NHL history. It would also prove to be the final goal of his illustrious career. In time his playoff-goal record would be surpassed by Wayne Gretzky, Jari Kurri, Mark Messier, Glenn Anderson, and Mike Bossy, most of whom would play many more games than Richard.

After 18 seasons Richard must have had retirement in mind when he skated in to retrieve the history-making puck. Five months later he would attend Montreal's fall training camp, score four or five goals in one of the early scrimmages, then walk into Frank Selke's office to announce that he would play no more.

In game four against Toronto, another fast start by Montreal left the Leafs frustrated and discouraged. Beliveau and Harvey scored goals 28 seconds apart in the first ten minutes and Jacques Plante recorded the shut-out in a 4–0 triumph. While the Habs drank from the Cup, fans predicted their winning streak would stretch into six, seven, even ten straight championships. At the time, there was no inkling that the early '60s would belong to the Blackhawks and the Leafs.

There was a modest victory celebration following the final game. Perhaps Doug Harvey said it for all the players when he told reporters, "When you win eight straight games in the playoffs and you win five Cups in a row, there's not a whole lot to get excited about."

By winning in the minimum number of games, the Canadiens equalled a record set by the Detroit Red Wings in the 1952 playoffs.

They Could Have Won Eight in a Row

For any NHL club to match or surpass the Montreal record of five straight Stanley Cups would take an incredible effort. It would be a tremendous feat. In the modern era of free agency and budget restraints, it's not likely to happen. Hockey dynasties may be a part of the past—like rovers and C forms and maskless goalies.

Talk to the players who helped fashion the Canadiens' five-year Stanley Cup streak, and they'll tell you, "Hey, it could have been eight."

Check it out; they're absolutely right. Montreal captured the Cup in 1953 (Elmer Lach scored the series-winning goal over Boston). The following spring, in 1954, the Habs lost to Detroit in seven games, on a fluke goal in overtime by Tony Leswick. The puck bounced off Doug Harvey's glove and into the Montreal net. If Lady Luck hadn't been riding on Leswick's shot, the Habs might have made it two in a row.

In 1955 the Habs were badly rattled by Rocket Richard's suspension for the playoffs. Still, they battled the Red Wings through seven games, losing the deciding game 3–1. Experts agreed the series could have gone either way and the Rocket's absence might have been the difference.

Then came the five Cups in a row from 1956 to 1960. In 1961 the first-place Habs took a run at a sixth consecutive Cup, starting with Chicago.

Despite injuries, the Habs were favoured to sweep the Hawks in the semis. Blake's men won the opener 6–2, then lost two close ones by 4–3 and 2–1 scores. The third game was decided after 52 minutes of overtime. Montreal rebounded with a 5–2 victory, outshooting Chicago 50–21. But Glenn Hall's goaltending led to back-to-back shutouts and the series was won by Chicago in six games. Two overtime goals by the Habs were disallowed in the series that Rocket Richard called "the dirtiest I've ever seen." Had the Habs won, they would have been arguably a better team than Detroit, upset winners over Toronto.

Fluke goals, injuries, hot goaltending, and disallowed goals in overtime can be applauded or cursed but they're all part of the game. Montreal fans who sigh and say, "If only this, or if only that, we might have won eight or even nine Cups in a row," might also keep in mind that rival fans, in Detroit perhaps, might be sighing, "If only this or that had happened for us, the damn Habs might never have won five straight Stanley Cups."

Rousseau's Strange Penalty Shot

It happened in 1960–61, during Bobby Rousseau's first year with Montreal. The Canadiens were playing the Boston Bruins at the Forum and Rousseau was awarded a penalty shot against Bruce Gamble, the Bruin netminder.

Traditionally, players taking a free shot move in close and either shoot for a corner or try to deke out the goalie. Not Rousseau. He tried something totally unexpected. He cradled the puck at centre ice, gathered speed, and suddenly unleashed a slapshot from 45 feet out—just inside the blue line. Gamble, taken by surprise, moved too late and the red light blinked on. Rousseau's blast remains the longest penalty-shot goal in NHL history.

Rousseau, despite being an excellent team player and a fine skater with a powerful shot, seldom received the attention he deserved. Perhaps it's because he avoided physical contact whenever possible. Or because he wore a helmet before they became commonplace.

"When I first broke in I didn't worry about getting hit," he once told me. "Then I discovered the hard checks I took slowed me down. Two or three stiff checks and I'd be drained by the end of the game. So I figured I'd simply avoid some of the big bodycheckers."

His frantic leaps to stay intact were not appreciated by many of the Forum faithful. They saw his style as lacking in courage. And they faulted his decision to wear a helmet.

"Look at this this way," Rousseau said at the time. "In pro football, all the players wear helmets. They don't have pucks and sticks flying around their heads. In hockey, a skate can slice you open and a skull can be fractured against the boards. Hockey players don't fall on nice, soft grass. They crash to the ice. Seems to me all hockey players should be wearing helmets."

One of 12 children of a factory supervisor in Ste. Hyacinthe, Quebec, Rousseau credits a bestselling book for his scoring success in the NHL—245 goals in 15 seasons with Montreal, Minnesota, and the New York Rangers.

"I picked up *The Power of Positive Thinking* during my third season in the league," he recalled. "And the book did wonders for me, helping me to have a great deal of confidence in my ability on the ice."

He must have been reading a chapter from the book before a game with Detroit one night at the Forum. It was February 1, 1964. His line was scored on during its first shift and Rousseau was determined to get a goal back. With a few seconds left in the first period, Bobby whipped a shot from 40 feet at Red Wing goalie Roger Crozier. Crozier blocked the puck but gave up a lengthy rebound. Rousseau whacked the puck again and this time it found the net.

Midway through the second period, Rousseau struck again, scoring on a screened shot from inside the blue line. Goal number two! Before the period ended, Henri Richard fed Rousseau a quick pass in front of the Red

Wing net. Crozier went down, Rousseau flicked the puck over him, and completed his hat trick—his first in the NHL. He tried to recover the puck but a frustrated Crozier shot it high over the boards into the crowd.

In the opening moments of the third period, Rousseau struck again, with a long shot that kept rising until it wound up behind Crozier. Minutes later, Gilles Tremblay kicked the puck across the crease to a waiting Rousseau and he slid the puck into the net. Five goals for the speedy Rousseau! Only one Canadien had scored more: Newsy Lalonde potted six in a 14–7 rout of Toronto back in 1920.

Selke Signs the Pocket Rocket

"A funny thing happened in our training camp back in '55," Frank Selke Sr. once told me. "In our scrimmages all the big fellows in camp were running at this little rookie, Henri Richard, the Rocket's kid brother. Henri was only 19, 15 years younger than Maurice, and he was so small. I thought surely he'd need a year or two of seasoning and I told Toe Blake he wasn't ready. But in camp Henri stood right up to the veterans. And when they tried to take the puck away from him, he simply wouldn't let them have it.

"Toe Blake urged me to sign him right away, so I did. I remember the Rocket acted as his brother's advisor because Henri spoke little English. I asked Maurice how much his brother wanted and he replied, 'He doesn't care about money. He just wants to play.' So I made him a pretty standard offer: a $2,000 signing bonus and $100 per game. Maurice turned to Henri and translated my offer. Henri simply nodded, reached for a pen, and signed a contract.

"When they were leaving, I called them back. I took the contract and changed the signing bonus to $5,000. Why? Well, I didn't want the Richards to say later that I hadn't treated them fairly. In my long career as Montreal's general manager, I was blessed with many great players. But game in and game out, Henri Richard was the most valuable player of them all."

Red Fisher Recalls a Great Game in Chicago

Red Fisher, a Hall-of-Fame sportswriter, has been following the fortunes of the Montreal Canadiens since the night of *L'affaire Richard*—the riot at the Montreal Forum on March 17, 1955. It was Fisher's first hockey assignment for the Montreal *Star*.

But that game does not rank at the top of Fisher's list of the most memorable contests he's witnessed. For the 1955 game was not a game at all, merely a period of hockey, at the end of which the game was forfeited to the Detroit Red Wings.

Fisher's most vivid memory of a single game—out of the thousands he's seen—focuses on the Chicago Stadium (now gone) and a playoff match between the Canadiens and the Blackhawks. The date was March 26, 1961.

Nobody anywhere that spring, except for a few diehards in Chicago, picked the Blackhawks to win their semifinal series with the mighty Canadiens. Montreal had finished atop the standings after the 70-game schedule with 41 victories and 92 points, 17 more than the Blackhawks, who'd won just 29 games.

Boom Boom Geoffrion (95 points) and Jean Beliveau (90 points) finished one-two in the scoring race, while Dickie Moore (69) and Henri Richard (68) also finished among the top ten scorers. Top scorer among the Blackhawks was Bill Hay (11th) with 11 goals and 59 points, although Bobby Hull and Stan Mikita were not far behind.

Even after the Blackhawks stunned the Canadiens by splitting the first two games at the Forum, nobody was talking about an upset.

But midway through that March 26 game in the Windy City, delirious

Hawks fans began dreaming of one. Chicago's Murray Balfour scored in the second period and late in the third it appeared the Hawks would win 1–0, a shutout for Glen Hall. Hall's brilliance had the fans—most of them in their shirtsleeves because of the intense heat—on their feet throughout the game.

Red Fisher recalls the final few seconds of the third period and wrote about it for the following day's paper:

Only 16 seconds left, and Canadiens are down to their last sigh. There's a faceoff to the right of Hall's net, and Canadiens have yanked Plante in favor of an extra attacker. Henri Richard is taking the faceoff, and Chicago's way is clear, right? Tie up Richard as soon as the puck is dropped. Tie him up in any way possible…legal, illegal, nothing mattered but to have time run out.

The puck is dropped, and Richard doesn't even bother trying to get it back to an associate. One stride, a small fake of his head, and Hall is beaten.

The screams in the stadium are stilled. Chicago fans look at one another numbly. It's as if their pockets had been picked by a stranger. How could this happen? So close…

Now it's one minute into the first overtime period, and the pain is really starting to show, because isn't that Richard again with the puck—this time on a breakaway from the blueline? Only Hall back…the fans are on their feet…many of them afraid to look. Then the heavy air is filled with high sounds again, because this time Hall stops Richard…and then it starts.

What started was a heart-gripping series of end-to-end rushes by both teams. Hall stops breakaways…Plante twists and leaps to stop the Hawks. Up and down…bodies clashing…the breath whistling through open mouths as players are crashed into the boards. Somehow soon, somebody had to get the goal that would bring this to a halt.

They played through the first overtime period, with a minimum of a half dozen brilliant scoring chances on each side. Hall and Plante stopped them all.

The players heaved their way into the second period, and by now the legs weren't moving quite as rapidly. But there's a scramble around the Chicago nets midway through the second overtime period and Don Marshall is reaching for a loose puck and then he's waving his stick wildly and hopping from one foot to another. Behind all, the red light is aglow.

But what's this? Even while the Canadiens are streaming off their bench to envelop Marshall in the embraces that hockey players have reserved for winners over the years, referee Dalton MacArthur is waving his arms from side to side. He's also shaking his head.

No goal!

Stick above the shoulder, insists MacArthur.

Have you ever heard 20,000 throats sigh with relief? The sound rose from the seats and even the fury of the Canadiens and shrieks from coach Toe Blake were lost.

Third overtime period! It's the same furious end-to-end rushes again. It was if the fury of the second overtime period had provided both teams with the energy they needed to go back to the speed and clash and clang of bodies again. Now it's a little beyond the 11-minute mark of the third overtime and Dickie Moore is sent to the penalty box. He sits there and hangs his head.

On the ice, though, the Hawks are aroused. They press into the Canadiens zone and there's a forest of bodies around Plante, all of them slashing at a loose puck. Murray Balfour gets to it first and now the light is aglow behind Plante. Chicago Stadium explodes as referee MacArthur skates toward the minor officials bench to report on the goal that had provided Chicago with a 2–1 victory after 52 minutes and 12 seconds of overtime.

One of the men watching MacArthur is behind the Canadiens bench, but coach Toe Blake isn't there for long. Even before MacArthur reaches the scorekeeper, Blake has pushed his way past several of his players on the far side of the rink and he slides and slips across the ice toward an unwary MacArthur. The referee is leaning over with a message to the score-keeper when Blake reaches him. The punch he throws lands on the referee's shoulder and as MacArthur starts in surprise, the fist deflects higher and catches him lightly on the jaw.

Bedlam!

Anybody who saw or appeared in that game will never forget it. The Canadiens came back to win game four in Chicago but lost the next two by 3–0 shutouts and were eliminated from the playoffs after five straight Stanley Cups.

Blake, it's certain, never forgot it. First of all, his team lost. Secondly, his punch cost him a $2,000 fine.

"And it wasn't even a decent punch," he sighed.

Hab Fan Steals the Cup

On the night of April 1, 1962, Ken Kilander, a 25-year-old Montrealer, created a few moments of hockey notoriety for himself with a brazen act of theft, one that saw his name and photo splashed across the sports pages everywhere.

It happened at the Chicago Stadium, late in a playoff game between the Canadiens and the Blackhawks. But wait, let's hear how Kilander described what happened.

In the sixties I used to follow the Habs around all the time. I'd finance my trips by playing piano in bars in most of the [Original Six] cities. I'd wear my Canadiens jacket and lots of times I'd travel on the same train as the players. Everybody knew me 'cause I'd been following the Canadiens for years, at home and on the road.

I was in the cocktail lounge of the LaSalle Hotel in Chicago that day and I was talking to some reporters who were covering the series. They were talking about the Stanley Cup and who might win it. One of them said Chicago was likely to knock Montreal out of the playoffs. Naturally, I got upset and told them that the Cup belongs in Montreal, nowhere else.

At that moment I knew where the Cup was—locked up in a showcase in the lobby of the Chicago Stadium. So I said to these guys, just kidding of course, "What would you fellows do if I went and got the Cup and brought it here to give to the Canadiens?"

One of them laughed and said, "Well, it is April Fools Day. If you go and steal the Cup I guarantee I'll take your picture and put your name in the paper." Another said, "What a story that would be. And what an uproar that would cause here in Chicago."

Nothing more was said but when I went to the game that night I walked by the Cup on display in the Chicago Stadium. I could tell right away that the lock on the glass case was a flimsy thing and easily broken.

I took my seat in the stands and watched the first two periods of play. My Habs were getting clobbered and halfway through the third period the Hawks led 4–1. I couldn't take any more of that.

I jumped out of my seat and ran down into the lobby to take another look at the Stanley Cup. There was nobody around so I pushed in on the glass and the lock gave way. I couldn't resist reaching in and taking the Cup in my arms. The Hawks were about to win [the semi-finals] and who knew when I'd ever see it again. The Cup meant everything to me.

I started carrying it across the lobby when an usher spotted me. He asked me what the hell I was doing and I said, "I'm taking the Cup back to Montreal where it belongs."

He did a fancy double take and then started yelling at the top of his lungs. "Stop him! Help! Some guy's stealing the Cup!" If he hadn't spotted me I might have got away with it. But his screams brought some policemen running and they grabbed me and arrested me before I could get very far. It's hard to run very fast when you're lugging the Stanley Cup.

The next morning I had to appear before a judge who looked very stern. He said to me, "You can go back to the Stadium tomorrow night and cheer all you want for your Canadiens. But the Cup stays here unless the Blackhawks lose which I doubt very much they will." Then he smiled at me and let me go.

The bad news was the Hawks did eliminate the Habs that season [only to lose the final series to Toronto]. The good news was the reporter was right about putting my picture in all the papers for my stunt did create a sensation. There were all kinds of write-ups about my botched attempt to run off with Lord Stanley's Cup. One guy even wrote that the Cup weighed 150 pounds and he couldn't understand how I lifted it with ease. But it doesn't weigh even fifty pounds. The whole thing was intended as a joke and looking back, I know what I did wasn't right. But I couldn't help it. I wanted the Canadiens to win so badly. I collected enough clippings from that incident to fill a scrapbook.

At least one NHL general manager didn't see the humour in Kilander's prank. "The Stanley Cup is a sacred thing," said Muzz Patrick of the New York Rangers. "The following season I barred the guy from Madison Square Garden. Then he came to me and pleaded with me to let him in to see a game against Montreal. I relented but I told him he couldn't wear his Montreal jacket. I'll say this for him—he's a hell of a piano player."

The Unlikely Vezina Winner

His friends smiled when Charlie Hodge talked about winning the Vezina Trophy. They figured he didn't have a chance.

This was back in the 1963–64 season when little Charlie was called on to replace the injured Gump Worsley in the Montreal goal. Brought up from the Quebec Aces, Hodge responded to the challenge and played one solid game after another. But the Vezina? That would go to Chicago's Glenn Hall, said the experts.

In those days the Vezina was awarded to the goalie playing for the team with the fewest goals against. At the halfway point, the Canadiens had given up 33 more goals than the Blackhawks, a huge disparity. If Hodge envisioned his name on the Vezina, he was dreaming. There are, however, no rules against dreams or fantasy in the NHL, and if Charlie indulged in moods of make-believe or stargazing, where was the harm? Two or three bad games would soon bring him back to reality. Face it, Charlie, you're just a backup, was the word from the fans.

Hodge didn't care what others thought. And he refused to be part of any high-scoring games. In fact, he got hot and compiled a shutout streak of 179 minutes. Suddenly, Hall's big goal advantage had evaporated.

On the final night of the season, Montreal played New York. The Canadiens needed a big effort against the Rangers if they hoped to capture first place and help their netminder win the Vezina. The game was a close one, tied 1–1 in the third period. Suddenly there was a checking breakdown and three Rangers raced in on Hodge. Rod Gilbert, one of the league's top scorers, wound up for a slapshot and Hodge flew out to cut down the angle. But Gilbert was faking. He skimmed a quick pass across to Camille Henry, his winger. Henry, thinking Gilbert would shoot, missed the pass and the puck flew into the corner.

Moments later, Boom Boom Geoffrion snared the puck and scored the winning goal for Montreal. The 2–1 triumph lifted the Habs into first place by one point over Chicago, and little Charlie Hodge had won the Vezina by the slimmest of margins, allowing 167 goals to Hall's 169.

Hodge later called the final game of the season "the highlight of my career."

Hodge had more big moments in hockey. The following season he played in 53 games and helped the Canadiens win the Stanley Cup. He also won another Vezina Trophy (with Gump Worsley) in 1965–66.

Fergie Feared Maiming an Opponent

John Ferguson played eight seasons with Montreal, from 1963–64 to 1970–71. He scored 145 goals in 500 games.

"Fergie, you could have played longer than you did," I mentioned to him once. "When you retired you talked about all the great business opportunities that were open to you. But isn't it true that the main reason you quit when you did was because you were afraid you were going to hurt someone on the ice?"

He gave me a long look. Then he said, "You've got that right. I was beginning to worry about doing some serious damage to someone."

Perhaps he was thinking of some of the young turks who had challenged him, only to wind up on the seat of their hockey pants, nursing a swollen jaw or a bloody lip. Or perhaps it was Eric Nesterenko who crossed his mind. Remember Eric, a tall winger with Chicago? In the Stanley Cup finals in 1965, Fergie and Nesterenko collided in a corner. They snarled at each other. Then Fergie's fist went "pop!" and the Chicago player folded to the ice. A couple of seasons later, they tangled again in the third period of a game. This time Fergie delivered three punches—"pop, pop, pop!"—and Nesterenko collapsed again. Fifteen minutes after the game the doctors were still attending to him where he lay on a table in the Blackhawk dressing room.

Writer Paul Rimstead once asked Fergie if Toe Blake ever sent him on the ice with instructions to fight a rival player. Fergie hesitated, then replied, "Never in front of the team. He'd take me aside and say, 'Listen, you'd better straighten that guy out.'

"I always knew what he meant."

It was an incident in a Western Hockey League game that helped start Ferguson en route to the heavyweight championship of the NHL. He was just a kid then, a stickboy for the Vancouver Canucks. During a rough game one night, the league's most-feared player, hardrock defenceman Larry Zeidel, fought the Canucks' Phil Maloney in front of the Vancouver bench. Fergie looked on, wide-eyed, as Zeidel pummelled his smaller opponent. The stick-boy was enraged when none of Maloney's teammates came to his rescue.

"From that moment, I hated the Canucks," Fergie would say later. "I vowed that would never happen with any team I might get to play for."

Years later, Ferguson made it to the American Hockey League with Cleveland. One night he encountered Zeidel, now a veteran of hundreds of hockey scraps. They dropped the gloves and squared off. Zeidel never knew what hit him as Fergie's punches left him bruised and bloody.

"Yeah, I felt good about that battle," Fergie said. "I gave him a few shots to make up for his treatment of Maloney."

One of Fergie's own teammates almost took a drubbing from him one night. When a pair of Habs began to get the worst of a punch-up in New York, Fergie leaped up on the bench and was about to go to their aid. A teammate grabbed him by the arm and said, "Fergie, why bother?"

Fergie shook loose and jumped into the fight. After serving a penalty he came back to the Montreal bench still seething—not at the Rangers but at the Canadien who'd told him not to bother. That player will never know how close he came to being punched out by one of his own teammates.

Fergie's ambition in hockey was not only to enjoy a lengthy career in the NHL but to forge a reputation as the meanest, rottenest player ever to perform in the league. There are many scarred oldtimers who played against him who are willing to step forward and testify that he fulfilled those ambitions admirably.

Hating an opponent was not a seasonal thing with Fergie. He carried ill feelings with him throughout the year. "When you were as mean as I was," he says, "you can't turn it on and off like a faucet. That's why I never rubbed elbows with players from other teams at banquets, summer schools, or on the golf course."

Despite his sometimes violent nature, John Ferguson was first and foremost a player. He performed hard and well and with the kind of emotion fans appreciate. Most Montrealers emphatically rank him as one of the most entertaining and popular players in the Habs' long history.

Fergie's First Game

Three mighty punches, two impressive goals, and a hard-earned assist. That terse summary describes John Ferguson's first game as a Montreal Canadien. On October 8, 1963, in his debut against the Boston Bruins at the Boston Garden, Ferguson played a huge role in the game's outcome and wasted no time in placing a massive fist in the face of the league's meanest, toughest player. By the end of the evening, the hard-nosed rookie was confident he'd be around for a long time.

Fergie had come up from Cleveland of the American Hockey League prior to that season, on the recommendation of Toe Blake, who'd scouted him and was impressed with his goal production (38) and his prowess as a fighter. The tough winger had had his choice of three NHL clubs: Montreal, Boston, or New York. Without hesitation, Fergie had picked Montreal. "I've dreamed of playing in a Canadiens' uniform ever since I was a kid," he said.

Manager Frank Selke signed Ferguson to a contract. It called for $8,000 a year whether he played in the NHL or in the minors. Ferguson had no agent to advise him and no qualms about signing. He felt he was so damn lucky to be invited to play for the best team in a six-team league that he grabbed the pen, ignored all the fine print, and scrawled his signature on the paper Selke pushed in front of him. In today's hockey marketplace, a character player like Ferguson would become an instant millionaire in the same situation.

It was coach Toe Blake who said to Ferguson before his Boston debut, "You'll be playing on a line with Beliveau and Geoffrion against the Bruins tonight. Don't let those Boston buggers bother my big scorers or push them around." It wasn't an order to clobber a couple of Bruins but it was the next thing to it.

Fergie vowed he'd be ready for any Bruin nastiness, especially if it stemmed from "Terrible Ted" Green, a mean-spirited defenceman with no fear of the Habs, a player with the heart and guts of a pit bull. Green had been Montreal property at one time and in his first training camp the 18-year-old had stunned everybody by flattening all three Richard brothers in a training camp scrimmage. Maurice and Henri Richard had been placed on a line with kid brother Claude and Green assaulted all three, pounding them to the ice. If he expected praise for his remarkable feat, he didn't get it. The Richards, like Elliot Ness, were all but untouchable. It was an unwritten rule. People looked at Green as if he'd just pole-axed three skating nuns. He was soon dispatched to the Boston Bruins.

Now, on opening night five years later, Green was lined up facing the Habs and the new kid, Ferguson, up from Cleveland, a threat to Green's moniker—"hockey's toughest player." The puck was dropped and Green, snarling defiance, moved up to intercept the rookie. A mere 12 seconds into the game they collided and the gloves flew off. Ferguson threw a solid right that landed in Green's nostrils. He followed up with a second well-aimed punch, and then a third furious blow. Green staggered back, shaken by the ferocity of Fergie's attack, his face numb from the punches. He realized instantly there was a new enforcer in the league, a deadly puncher who would bring grief to all who challenged him.

But Ferguson had more to prove that night. He wanted to show that the hands he used to knock opponents bow-legged could also cradle a hockey stick and control a speeding puck. In the first period, he took a pass from Beliveau and whacked home his first NHL goal, a rising shot over Eddie Johnston's shoulder. In the second period, with Green in the penalty box, Ferguson worked the power play and skimmed another goal past Johnston. A few minutes later, he helped set up the tying goal by Geoffrion. The game ended in a 4–4 deadlock and Ferguson skated off with the plaudits of his teammates and his coach ringing in his ears. Two goals and one assist, plus the satisfaction of humiliating the toughest man in hockey, "Terrible Ted" Green.

If there had been any doubt about Ferguson's ability to stick with the Canadiens, it was dispelled in the first 60 minutes—some might say the first 12 seconds—of his NHL career.

Fergie and the Golden Jet

On a summer's day not long ago, I was playing golf in a foursome that included John Ferguson. It was one of those celebrity scrambles that have become so popular in recent years. After several holes we approached the tee to a splendid par-three. On the tee swinging a club was a familiar figure: Bobby Hull. Hull's role that day was to shake hands and make small talk with the golfers, most of whom were delighted to meet him. He would tee off with them, then wait for the next foursome to come by.

Hull flashed his famous grin for our group and greeted us warmly. He turned to Fergie and said a few words—something like "Great weather, eh?"—and Fergie mumbled a reply as he teed up his ball. Then we were on our way again. I said, "Fergie, you and Bobby didn't spend much time conversing." He gave me a look and said, "That's probably the longest conversation I've ever had with him. We never got along too well."

When they played against each other in the NHL, Fergie showed little respect for the Golden Jet. He concedes that Hull was a brilliant offensive threat but, in his opinion, Hull didn't know the meaning of backchecking or defensive play.

He recalled two battles he had with Hull and wrote about both in his book *Thunder and Lightning.* At the Forum one evening, he charged at Hull and put a hard shoulder into his face. Hull went down, bleeding from a cut. Then he leaped up and threw three quick punches at Fergie. Fergie threw off his gloves and retaliated. He was incensed when he drew a five-minute penalty for crosschecking ("It was my shoulder that did the damage," he states), a ten-minute misconduct, and a $50 fine. He was further maddened when Chicago coach Billy Reay said, "It's disgraceful that Bobby had to take something like that from a two-bit player like Ferguson."

The next time the two collided, Hull was recuperating from a broken jaw and was wearing a protective cage attached to a helmet. Fergie credited Hull for showing courage and a willingness to fight but added, "He shouldn't have expected preferential treatment because of his injury." There was a scramble and out of it came Hull and Fergie, pushing and shoving. Fergie shoved Hull to his knees and drew back his fist. Before he could unload a haymaker, a voice cautioned him, "Hit him, Fergie, and the fans will think you're the biggest rat in hockey." He never threw the punch. Even so, he was ripped in the media for even shoving the Golden Jet, the most popular player of his era.

Fergie tells of an unusual postscript to that encounter. Hours later, he was walking through the airport when a woman approached him and said,

"Thank you for teaching my husband a lesson." Fergie didn't know the woman but was told by someone it was Joanne Hull, Bobby's wife. The Hulls went through a stormy divorce sometime later. "She made me a millionaire," Bobby would say at banquets. "The trouble is, I started with three million."

In his career with Montreal (1963 to 1971), Fergie served 1,214 minutes in penalties. Is there one infraction, I asked, that quickly comes to mind, and why is it memorable? He laughed. "Yeah, Frank Udvari gave me a two-minute minor one night for 'equipment falling to the ice.' It was unbelievable. I'd never heard of such a penalty. My jockstrap came loose and the cup fell through my pants and onto the ice. I was so embarrassed I didn't even argue with him."

Little-Known Facts About Fergie

When John Ferguson reigned as the NHL heavyweight champ, he considered an offer to fight George Chuvalo, the Canadian heavyweight champion. The three-round bout was to be staged at the Canadian National Exhibition grounds in Toronto. "I was really eager to do it," Fergie told me recently. "But when I asked Sam Pollock for permission, he said, 'Are you crazy? There's no bleepin' way I'm going to let you get in the ring with Chuvalo.'"

Fergie, who began his sports career as a lacrosse goalie, wanted to play for a professional lacrosse team I owned back in the '60s—the Montreal Canadiens. His skills in lacrosse were legendary. Again, Sam Pollock nixed the idea. But Fergie did serve with distinction as coach and manager of the team.

His wife, Joan, is the only girl Fergie ever went out with. They met in Grade 7.

He is always well dressed and never wears the same suit two days in a row. If the Habs lost a game, he would never wear the suit he had on to another game.

On the day of a game, he thought of nothing but hockey. His focus on the game was absolute, almost as though he were in a trance. Even in retirement, playing oldtimers' hockey, he seldom spoke to an opposing player.

He abhorred the thought of shaking hands with an opponent after a game. "That kind of guy will never be a winner," he says. "Why congratulate a guy who's taking money out of your pocket. A pro is supposed to do one thing and that's win."

One night Fergie, nursing an injury, was watching a game from the press box. A rival player knocked a Canadien to the ice and stood over him, daring the rest of the Habs to do anything about it. Fergie leaped from his seat, grabbed the chair, and threw it across the press box. Then he stormed out.

Monahan's NHL Debut

The first player selected in the initial draft of amateur talent was a 16-year-old centre from the St. Michael's College Juveniles in Toronto. The year was 1963 and the drafting club was Montreal.

In the era of the Original Six, most of the top prospects were already the property of NHL clubs and the draft was a novelty. Only 21 players were plucked from the amateur ranks and Garry Monahan's name topped the list. During the 1967–68 season he found himself sitting on the end of the Montreal bench enjoying his first NHL game.

It was at the Forum against Boston and he never expected to get any ice time. Suddenly he felt a tap on the shoulder and he leaped over the boards for his first NHL shift. The puck came right to him and he darted in behind the net with it. Barrelling down on him was the Bruins' Eddie Shack. Just before they collided and fell in a heap, Monahan fired the puck along the boards to teammate Mickey Redmond.

Redmond, unable to clear the puck out of the zone, slapped it right back in behind the net. The flying puck struck Monahan on the head and knocked him unconscious. When he came to his senses, revived by smelling salts, he was back in the dressing room, finished for the night.

"The odd thing was, Shack got a five-minute penalty on the play," Monahan recalled. "The ref didn't see Mickey's shot hit me but he did see the blood that flowed from the wound. He figured Shack was responsible and gave him a major penalty. That's about all I remember of my NHL debut with the Canadiens."

Monahan played in only 14 games over two seasons for Montreal but he spent another decade in the league, playing for Detroit, Los Angeles, Toronto, and Vancouver.

Dennis Hull's Forum Memories

"Early in my career, I think it was 1964, I did something at the Forum one night that I've regretted for over 30 years. I slashed the great Jean Beliveau.

"My brother Bobby and I were playing for Chicago this night and Beliveau got a partial breakaway—with only Pierre Pilote standing between Beliveau and Glenn Hall, our goalie. As Pierre turned to go back, he fell down, leaving Jean a clear route to the net. I hustled over as fast as I could and I laid the lumber on him. I hit him as hard as I could with my stick, right across the arms. But Beliveau kept moving and flipped the puck in behind Hall for a goal.

"Then he wheeled around the net and came right up to me. He gave me a look—I'll never forget it—and said, 'I did not expect that kind of thing from you, Dennis.' He looked so hurt and disappointed in me that I felt like hiding under the logo at centre ice. I chased after him and apologized. 'Geez, I'm sorry, Jean. I'll never do that again.' He didn't look back and I wasn't sure he heard me so I said it louder. 'Jean, I'm really sorry. It won't happen again.'

"Meanwhile Billy Reay, our coach, wanted to know what the hell was going on. I told him I was apologizing to Jean Beliveau.

"'Jesus, you don't ever go around apologizing to guys,' he snorted.

"I said to him, 'But that's Jean Beliveau. One of my boyhood heroes.'

"Billy glared at me and said, 'What the hell does that have to do with anything? You never apologize.'

"I said, 'Okay, Billy.' But I was glad I did apologize because I felt awful about hitting Beliveau with that two-hander. It was the first and last one he ever got from me."

Dennis talks about his late father, Robert Hull, and how he enjoyed visiting the Forum for games there when his two sons starred for Chicago. One night the senior Hull took Dennis aside before an important game against the Habs. "My dad put a big hand on my shoulder and looked as though he was about to deliver one of those father-to-son pep talks.

"Then he looked me right in the eye and he said, 'Dennis, you know what happens here in Montreal when the Canadiens score a big goal? The fans go wild and throw everything on the ice, including dozens of toe rubbers.'

"I said, 'Yeah, I know, Dad,' wondering what he was getting at.

"And he said, 'Well, tonight, when Beliveau or Richard scores, and everything comes flying out of the stands, I want you to fetch me a good pair of toe rubbers. Get me a size ten.'"

Dennis says, "And he was serious, too! Hey, this is a true story."

"Did you get him the toe rubbers?" I ask.

"Yeah, I did," chuckles Dennis. "I got him two pretty good size tens. Almost brand new. Trouble is, they were both lefts."

"I remember when Rocket Richard would attend most of our games at the Forum and he would sometimes shout at my brother Bobby as we were skating off at the end of a period.

"'Hey, Bob-bee,' he once shouted, 'you score 50 goals but you no score dem in 50 games lak I did.' Things like that.

"And Bobby, well, you know Bobby, he'd never argue about something like that. He'd shout back, 'You're absolutely right, Rocket. You were always a better scorer than I'll ever be. No doubt about that.'

"I guess that surprised the Rocket, because the next time we were leaving the ice he started to yell, 'Hey, Bob-bee, I tell you something else...'

"When Bobby grinned up at him I guess Rocket didn't know what he wanted to say. So he yelled down, 'Listen, Bob-bee, someday you gonna be old and fat lak me!'"

Somebody mentioned that Vladislav Tretiak often cited the New Year's Eve game in 1975 as his proudest moment as a hockey goalie. The game ended in a 3–3 tie and was one of the most thrilling games ever played.

Dennis Hull says that having Tretiak pay tribute to him was one of his most memorable moments in hockey. "You know the Russians have this ancient tradition of kissing their comrades on both cheeks," he says. "Tretiak greeted me in this manner at the Forum one day before a practice and I was both honoured and surprised. Honoured because he thought so highly of me and surprised because I happened to be tying my skates up at the time."

A Few Words About Moore

One can hardly leave the Toe Blake era without mentioning star left winger Dickie Moore, who, despite bad knees and bad shoulders, was a true Montreal superstar for most of his dozen years with the Habs. He played on six championship teams and an equal number of Cup winners. He joined the Habs midway through the 1951–52 season and averaged a point a game in 33 games. At that clip, he would have surpassed teammate Bernie Geoffrion in points, had he played the full season as Geoffrion did. And Geoffrion won the Calder Trophy as top rookie that season. In 1958–59 Moore won the NHL scoring title over teammate Jean Beliveau (96 points to 91). A year earlier he won it over Henri Richard (84 to 80). Moore retired to nurse his aching joints in 1963.

He made two comebacks, with Toronto in 1964–65—the Toronto trainer said Moore's knees were the worst he'd ever seen—and with St. Louis in 1967–68. When St. Louis made it all the way to the Stanley Cup finals in 1968, Moore played like a 20-year-old in the postseason, notching seven goals and seven assists. He limped away from the game after the Blues lost the Cup final to the Habs in four games. He became quite a successful businessman in Montreal following his playing days and was a frequent guest on our Hockey Night in Canada telecasts out of the Forum.

Chapter 6
SIX CUPS IN THE SEVENTIES

Scotty Bowman: Often an Enigma

In the spring of 1971, in a Montreal restaurant, I approached Scotty Bowman, then coach of the St. Louis Blues, and requested an interview.

"Scotty, I'm planning a book about a variety of careers in hockey and I'd like your comments about the role of a general manager," I told him.

Scotty hesitated a moment, then smiled at his three luncheon companions. He rose from the table and said to me, "Come with me."

He led me to a quiet corner, where he said, "Brian, this is an awkward time for that kind of interview. This is off the record but I may not be with the Blues much longer."

I was astonished. There'd been nothing in the papers, no rumours. I stammered, "Really?"

He smiled. "So let's see what happens in St. Louis and we can do it another time, okay?"

I said, "Fine with me, Scotty." I was surprised, not so much at learning that Bowman's future in St. Louis was iffy as that he'd confided in me. I didn't know Bowman very well and I was amazed that he trusted me to keep his revelation confidential.

Shortly after our chat, Bowman, despite leading the Blues to three Stanley Cup finals from 1968 to 1970, had a major confrontation with the Blues' owners and was fired.

That was the season the Montreal Canadiens won the Stanley Cup under coach Al MacNeil. But MacNeil couldn't possibly survive in Montreal—not as coach, and not with the French press—after Henri Richard had roasted him in the 1971 playoffs.

MacNeil was dispatched to Halifax to coach the Habs' AHL farm club and before the door closed behind him, Sam Pollock was on the phone to Scotty Bowman, his first choice to replace MacNeil.

Bowman jumped at the opportunity to return to Montreal. He had begun his hockey career with the Canadiens organization in 1954, as an assistant to Pollock, then manager of the Hull-Ottawa Junior Habs. Prior to the 1967–68 season, with the NHL about to double in size, Bowman moved up to the St. Louis Blues, soon replaced Lynn Patrick as coach, and guided the Blues to the Stanley Cup finals for the next three seasons.

Bowman's greatest coaching successes came after he donned his Montreal cap. In eight seasons the teams he coached captured five Stanley Cups. From 1975–76 through 1978–79 his teams were the class of the NHL, winning 229 games while losing a mere 46. During the 1976–77 season Bowman's Habs won a record 60 games of 80 played and lost only 8. It was a mark that stood until the 1995–96 campaign, when Detroit, another Bowman-coached team, captured 62 wins in the 82-game schedule.

Bowman is the winningest coach in NHL history, has seven Stanley Cup rings, and has already been inducted into the Hockey Hall of Fame. He is in his 25th season as an NHL coach and has piloted teams to six Cup triumphs. He hopes to become the only man to win the Cup with three different teams (Montreal, Pittsburgh, and Detroit) and he'd like to stay around to equal or break Toe Blake's coaching record of eight Stanley Cup championships.

In seven of his eight seasons with Montreal, the Habs notched more than 100 points; they missed the mark once with 99. His 1976–77 squad holds the NHL record for the fewest defeats (8) in a season of 70 or more games.

"Hockey is a game of discipline and patience," he says. "Play in your own end is so important. Good teams forecheck and sustain pressure on the other team."

When I worked with Scotty for several seasons on *Hockey Night in Canada*, I was amazed by his total focus on hockey. When I joined him on Saturday mornings at the Forum to watch the teams work out, I might greet him by saying, "Geez, Scotty, did you see the traffic jam outside? A water main burst and there are cars backed up in all directions . . ."

He'd stare at me with that deadpan look and reply, "Boston won again last night, eh?"

I'd say, "Yeah, but that traffic! And the cabbie got in a fight with the driver ahead of us…"

Scotty would say, "Montreal's power play hasn't looked good. They can't win if it doesn't improve…"

I could mention personal frustrations, erupting volcanoes, wars, or wages and Bowman would always steer the conversation back to what really mattered: hockey.

The hockey bug nipped at him early in life and, as a teenager, he was an excellent prospect for the NHL. That was before he encountered Jean-Guy Talbot in a game in Montreal. Bowman had whizzed around the lanky defence-man to score a pair of goals and Talbot vowed it wouldn't happen a third time. When Bowman attacked again, Talbot whacked him over his unprotected head with a two-hander, ending his career. The wound to Bowman's head required over 40 stitches and the injury was so severe that surgeons inserted a metal plate in Bowman's skull. Talbot went on to play over a thousand games in the NHL and was on seven Stanley Cup winners with the Canadiens. Bowman's injury forced him to give up the game he loved to play.

If Bowman fumed over the unfairness of it all, he never let on. Seventeen seasons after his injury, Bowman, then coaching St. Louis, heard that

Jean-Guy Talbot had been released by the Detroit Red Wings. Without a moment's hesitation, he claimed his old antagonist for the Blues.

Prior to the 1978–79 season, when Sam Pollock retired as the Habs' general manager, Scotty Bowman was regarded as the logical successor. When the position went to Irving Grundman, an outsider who listed his sports credentials as owner of a bowling establishment, Bowman was peeved. He stayed with Montreal one more season, won another Stanley Cup, then announced his departure. His disdain for the man who knew more about strikes and spares than goals and assists was verbalized.

"There is no room on the Canadiens for myself and Irving Grundman," he told reporters. "It got to the point where it was either him or me. There were far too many differences of opinion. Let's be blunt about it. I respect him as a businessman, but I have no respect for him as a hockey man. It is best for both of us that I leave, and best for the hockey team."

Bowman confirmed he would be leaving Montreal to accept the position of general manager of the Buffalo Sabres.

Bowman left with tongues wagging about his coaching tactics, for his methods were often controversial.

Terry Harper: "I couldn't stand him. I couldn't play under him any more. Life is too short for such nonsense." Harper declined a three-year contract extension and welcomed a trade to Los Angeles in 1972. "In Montreal it would mean three more years of high-priced hell," he said.

When Bowman was rescued from a hotel fire in St. Louis by his players (J. C. Tremblay commandeered a ladder from the inept local fire brigade and hauled Bowman off a balcony), Pierre Bouchard quipped, "Next time we'll bring marshmallows." There were cheers when it was learned Bowman had lost his notebook containing for and against records of his players.

Ken Dryden (in *The Game*): "Scotty Bowman is not someone who is easy to like. He does not slap backs, punch arms, or grab elbows. He is shy and not very friendly. Abrupt, straightforward, sometimes obnoxious, controversial, but never colourful. He is not Vince Lombardi, tough and gruff with a heart of gold. Someone might say of him, as former Packers great Henry Jordon said of Lombardi, 'He treats us all the same—like dogs,' but he doesn't. He plays favourites. His favourites, while rarely feeling favoured, are those who work and produce for him. He is complex, confusing, misunderstood, unclear in every way but one. He is a brilliant coach, the best of his time."

Some of Bowman's players complained that he once entered their hotel rooms secretly and checked around for bottles of booze.

Tiger Williams, playing for Vancouver against Buffalo in the 1980 playoffs, knocked Bowman cold with a two-hander while all eyes were on an injured Sabre player in the corner of the rink.

Sabre defenceman Gerry Korab, when he heard Bowman was coming to Buffalo, told me, "I'm gone. I once spit on him for things he said about me from the Montreal bench."

Me? I like the guy. He says kind words about my books and sends me Christmas cards every year. But then, I never had to play for him.

Houle Was a Great Junior

When Rejean Houle was 20 years old, he could look back on a junior-hockey career that was truly phenomenal. In 1969, following his final season with the Montreal Junior Canadiens, he captured the Red Tilson Trophy as MVP of the Ontario Hockey Association's powerful Junior A League. Then he was awarded the Max Kaminsky Memorial Trophy, which is roughly equivalent to the NHL's Lady Byng Trophy. He led the league in scoring and was named to the All-Star team. Players who finished behind him in the balloting for the Tilson award included Darryl Sittler, Marcel Dionne, Gilbert Perreault, and Rick MacLeish.

Houle was lauded by all the major-league coaches and managers as the outstanding junior player in Canada and was, of course, the first draft choice of the Montreal Canadiens in 1969. Note: It was the final year when Montreal had access to the top two French-Canadian junior players. Their second draft choice was Marc Tardif, Houle's teammate.

That season Houle captained one of the greatest junior clubs ever assembled. His mates included Gilbert Perreault, Richard Martin, Jocelyn Goevremont, J. P. Bordeleau, and diminutive Bobby Lalonde.

"We had an incredible team," Lalonde said recently, "and sometimes we drew bigger crowds at the Forum than the Canadiens. We couldn't go anywhere without being recognized. I turned down a $5,000 bonus offer to play with another team just so I could play with Houle, Tardif, and the others."

Houle recalls how nervous he was when he first joined Montreal. "I was shaking the first time I entered the famous dressing room. Then I found out my locker was right between Jean Beliveau and Henri Richard. I was so much in awe of those two I could barely speak. But they were so good to me. They made me feel like I was part of the team right away."

Dennis Hull, the former Blackhawk star, can testify to Houle's excitement over making it to the NHL. "We played in Montreal one night and after the game we were sitting on the team bus parked outside the Forum. We were waiting for the stragglers to climb aboard when I noticed Rejean Houle jump on the bus and look down the aisle. I shouted, 'Hey, Rejean, you're on the wrong bus.' And he shouted back, 'No, I'm not. I'm here to get your brother's autograph.'"

After three seasons with the Canadiens and two Stanley Cup victories, Houle jumped to Quebec of the WHA. He had been used sparingly and in a checking role with the Habs and he wanted to prove himself as a scorer in the rival league. Besides, Quebec City had offered him about four times the money he was making in Montreal. In Quebec he became a star and a 50-goal scorer.

After three seasons as a Nordique, he was happy to return to the Canadiens in 1976–77, just in time to play on three straight Stanley Cup teams. "Those were wonderful years," he says. "Sam Pollock and Scotty Bowman put together the most complete team I have ever seen with players like Ken Dryden and Guy Lafleur at the very top of their games."

In those heady days, Houle had no idea of what he would do with his life after hockey. "I was a good student in school," he told a *Hockey News* reporter. "Always at the top of my class. Then I quit after Grade XI to play hockey."

At age 33 he retired from the game, thankful for an opportunity to join Molson's in a public-relations role. He became a loyal company man, highly regarded for his organizational skills. But who would have guessed that one day he'd be handpicked by Ron Corey and ushered into the manager's office once occupied by Hall-of-Fame legends like Pollock, Selke, and Savard?

Beliveau Credited for Unique Cup Tradition

During Jean Beliveau's playing career, the Canadiens made the Stanley Cup playoffs 17 times and captured the gleaming trophy on ten occasions. In 1970–71, after the Habs ousted the Blackhawks in the seventh game of the final series in Chicago, league president Clarence Campbell presented the silverware to team captain Beliveau.

Knowing that he was about to retire, and aware that he would never enjoy such a moment again, Beliveau did something quite extraordinary. He raised the Cup in triumph and then began a leisurely skate around the ice, holding the Cup aloft for all to see. The Chicago fans, bitterly disappointed that their club had lost, began to smile and applaud. Many of them stood. It was as if they sensed what Beliveau was trying to say to them: "It is not merely our victory but yours as well. We all share the joy of hockey and a passion for the game. For it is a superb game, one that all fans cherish. And this Cup symbolizes its glorious tradition."

Some oldtimers recall the Red Wings skating around with the Cup several years earlier, but it was Beliveau who put his signature on what is now a familiar tradition. It seems fitting that a man who ranks as one of the game's greatest performers, and perhaps its best-loved sportsman, should introduce to the season finale the circling of the ice with the Cup held high. Thanks to Jean, the parade of joyous winners, with one member of the champions passing the trophy to another, has become the most popular part of the annual series-winning celebration.

Former Blackhawk Dan Maloney was a rookie when Beliveau hoisted the Cup over his shoulders in '71. "I'll never forget a goal I saw him score," Maloney told me recently. "There was a faceoff in the Chicago end to the right of Tony Esposito. We lined up against Beliveau, Yvan Cournoyer, and Gilles Tremblay. Pit Martin was our centreman facing Beliveau. When the linesman dropped the puck, Beliveau shot it in mid-air. It never hit the ice. He drilled that puck over Tony's shoulder so fast I couldn't believe it. It's the only time I ever saw such a goal."

Fans often wonder why it took the Habs so long to lure Beliveau into their fold. They've heard the oft-repeated story of how Beliveau, after his junior career, stayed on in Quebec City because he "owed it to the fans there." And how Montreal bought the entire Quebec Senior League and turned it pro in order to get Beliveau's signature on a contract. Recently another story surfaced. In the '50s a Quebec provincial cabinet minister is said to have informed the Canadiens that if they took Beliveau out of Quebec City before the expensive new arena there had been paid for, the Montreal Forum would be condemned because it didn't meet fire-regulation standards.

MacNeil Under Fire

After their stunning defeat of the Boston Bruins in the 1971 playoffs, the Canadiens remained hot and ousted the Minnesota North Stars in six games in the follow-up series. It was in this series that resentment simmered in the Montreal dressing room, much of it directed toward coach Al MacNeil. John Ferguson, never one to hide his feelings, was one Hab who vehemently disagreed with MacNeil's coaching style. Dryden appeared to be oblivious to the tension (more probably he chose to ignore it) and continued to play superbly.

In the final series with Chicago, Dryden felt the full power of Bobby and Dennis Hull's famed slapshots for the first time, and they stung his body right through his heavy equipment.

With the series tied 2–2, MacNeil benched Henri Richard for long stretches in game five and the Pocket Rocket exploded in a postgame interview. He told reporters, "He's the worst coach I ever played for."

Richard's outburst created a storm of controversy. The French media supported Richard, a huge hockey hero, in his condemnation of the anglo MacNeil. Reaction was so strong that MacNeil received several death threats and the Montreal bench had several bodyguards near it when the Habs defeated Chicago at the Forum in game six.

Later, Richard would say he regretted ripping into his coach because MacNeil was "a pretty good guy." Richard told Dick Irvin in 1991, "They made a lot about that in the newspapers. Even Guy Lafleur wrote about it in his book. Guy said I told MacNeil that he shouldn't be coach of the Canadiens because he couldn't speak French, and all that shit. I never said that in my life."

In game seven at Chicago, the Blackhawks jumped into a 2–0 lead. Then a tired Jacques Lemaire, striving for a line change, blasted a long shot from just over centre ice and headed for the bench. Incredibly, Lemaire's blast somehow skipped past Chicago goalie Tony Esposito. Then Henri Richard moved in and beat Esposito to tie the score.

In the third period, Richard danced around Keith Magnuson and whipped in what proved to be the winning goal. Richard would call his goals "two of the most memorable of my career."

At the end, the red carpet was rolled out and the Stanley Cup was lifted aloft by Jean Beliveau and the conquering Canadiens. "I knew it was the last time for me," Beliveau would say. "I was ready to step aside in my 40th year. And what a great way to go out, holding up another Stanley Cup."

Lafleur Cried over a Million-Dollar Deal

In 1972 fans showed more interest in hockey players' salaries than their game stats. Bobby Hull jumped to the Winnipeg Jets for a million dollars. Derek Sanderson, who was holding out for $80,000 a year from the Bruins (he'd earned $75,000 a year earlier) was flabbergasted when the Philadelphia Blazers shoved a $2.6-million contract in front of him. When he signed it, he became the highest paid athlete in the world. The following season, Mark Tardif and Rejean Houle left the Canadiens for the new league, accepting offers they simply couldn't refuse.

Guy Lafleur, having completed two NHL seasons (with 29 and 28 goals), was in a quandary. Should he leap to the WHA and the Quebec Nordiques, where his future father-in-law was an executive and where he was still idolized from his junior hockey days? Or should he sign a new contract with Sam Pollock (Lafleur's first contract would soon expire) and hope that the superstardom predicted for him would soon arrive? While he agonized over these decisions, he was also highly emotional because of another factor in his life: his impending marriage to Lise Barre.

Guy had heard the comments and read the papers about his worth as a player. Some commentators said he would never reach the heights of Jean Beliveau, the man he idolized, or even his junior rival, the little fireplug Marcel Dionne.

Montreal manager Sam Pollock was afraid that Lafleur might easily be persuaded to join the Nordiques. Pollock huddled with Gerry Patterson, Lafleur's agent, and proffered a new contract, one that called for a million dollars over the next ten years.

Patterson was elated and congratulated his young client on his good fortune.

"It's a great contract, Guy," he said. "And the deal can be renegotiated after three years and again after six years. I think you should sign it."

"What about the Quebec offer?" asked Lafleur.

"Their first offer was insulting," Patterson said. "And a second offer contained no guarantee. If you are injured or don't perform to expectations, they don't have to live up to it."

"But my future father-in-law tells me they are preparing a third offer. Shouldn't we wait to see it? And I want to talk about all of this with Lise. But she's out of town."

"Sam wants the contract signed today, Guy. Tomorrow at the latest. You've got a playoff game tomorrow night [against Buffalo] and it would be nice to get this out of the way."

Persuaded that the Montreal offer was the best he'd be able to get, Lafleur decided to sign the contract the following day.

According to Guy's biographer, following the game against the Sabres, Guy met with Roger Barre, who'd driven in from Quebec City. Unaware that Guy had signed Pollock's contract, Barre said, "Guy, the Nordiques are willing to pay you a million dollars over five years. And the contract is renegotiable after three seasons."

Barre was astonished when Guy burst into tears. His son-in-law-to-be was distraught. He'd just signed a contract for half a million dollars less than what Barre was proposing. And he'd done it despite an inner voice that had said wait, wait a few days.

In his book *Overtime: The Legend of Guy Lafleur*, author Georges-Hebert Germain writes of the above incident and a pleasant aftermath. After Lafleur's wedding a few weeks later, Roger Barre approached Gerry Patterson at the reception. "Gerry," he said, "I hope you've made a good decision for Guy because he's just committed himself for a long, long time."

Patterson replied, "Me? I assure you, Mr. Barre, I had nothing to do with it. It was Guy who decided to marry your daughter."

Barre laughed. So did daughter Lise and son-in-law Guy Lafleur.

Recently I talked with Gerry Patterson about this long-ago negotiation. His recollection of events differs from that of Germain. Patterson said, "The Nordiques' original offer to Guy was a three-year contract of $90,000 a year, plus a $50,000 signing bonus. Guy was not impressed with the figures because I had made him aware that Gerry Cheevers had left Boston for Cleveland of the WHA for $200,000 a year. The Quebec offer was peanuts. I suggested that Quebec review their position and submit their final best offer. The same opportunity would be given to the Canadiens.

"The final offer from Quebec was a $465,000, three-year package paying a $60,000 signing bonus plus $125,000, $135,000, and $145,000 for each of the three years. But the Nordiques were prepared to guarantee only $250,000 of the total, they wanted to share in Guy's future endorsement income, and they were not prepared to offer any performance bonuses beyond his basic salary.

"Sam Pollock, on the other hand, told me he had an excellent offer for Guy, one so good he wanted it signed within 24 hours. The offer was a ten-year, million-dollar contract plus signing bonus, plus performance bonuses, fully guaranteed, fully insured, and with the right to renegotiate at the end of three years and again at the end of six years. Sam also agreed to take out a one-million-dollar insurance policy on Guy's life. The package was instant security. The next night Sam and I met Guy just before he skated out for a playoff game against Buffalo. He signed the contract and the signing was announced minutes later in the Forum press lounge. When word reached Quebec City, it was like a day of mourning in that city. Marius Fortier, general manager of the Nordiques, said, 'Patterson did not act in the best interests of his client by signing a multi-year contract with the Canadiens.'

"There was no third offer from Quebec. It wasn't at all like the Gordie Howe deal in Houston, where the league guaranteed the Howes their money."

Lafleur defended Patterson at the time, saying, "I am the happiest guy on earth. The complete guarantee of the salary made the difference. If you know Gerry at all you will know that he deals with all the cards on the table. I have made this decision and I know full well what I am doing."

Ironically, Guy Lafleur's swan song in pro hockey took place in Quebec City at the end of the 1990–91 season—18 years after his momentous decision to stay with the Habs. And he bowed out with 15,000 fans thundering "Guy, Guy, Guy" in a pregame salute that never seemed to end. The league's two-time MVP, three-time scoring champ, and only playing member of the Hockey Hall of Fame ended his 17-year career after two seasons as a Nordique with 560 career goals and 1,353 points. His 560th goal came in a 4–3 loss to the Canadiens at the Forum the previous night. "Montreal fans gave him at least a five-minute ovation for that," said Steven Finn of the Nordiques. "And you can bet they timed the ovation back in Quebec City and resolved to make their tribute to Guy last a lot longer." Lafleur played on five Stanley Cup winners, all with Montreal.

For many seasons he was the best on the ice, the most explosive scorer in the game. He had pride and panache, a hunger to excel, and a flair for the spectacular, masking inner demons of anger and torment. His penchant for late-night celebrating, the smoking habit he couldn't shake, the fast cars he loved, all caused his friends and employers much concern. He chose his lifestyle, as superstars like Bobby Hull, Babe Ruth, and other athletic marvels are often allowed to do. And when he performed superbly, season after season, who would dare suggest he change? He was not a witty Shutt, a studious Dryden, or a diplomatic Beliveau. He was the Flower—warts and wondrous talents right up front. He was the Hab who lit up the '70s.

Brother Against Brother

There have been many brother acts in the NHL and many brothers who've played against brothers. On December 1, 1940, there were four sets of brothers on the ice when the New York Rangers met the Chicago Blackhawks. Lynn and Muzz Patrick and Neil and Mac Colville toiled for New York, while Max and Doug Bentley and Bill and Bob Carse performed for Chicago.

Most fans have forgotten that Gordie Howe's brother Vic played briefly in the NHL (33 games and three goals with the Rangers from 1950 to 1955). Gordie's sons Mark and Marty were another NHL brother combo. How many are aware that Wayne Gretzky's brother Brent scored one goal in a ten-game trial with Tampa Bay in 1993–94? Can't you hear Brent telling his children unashamedly, "Yes, your uncle Wayne and I clicked for about a thousand goals in the NHL"?

The fact that Louis Sutter of Viking, Alberta, sired six sons who became NHLers is truly astonishing. Among them they have accounted for more than 1,200 goals—and still counting!

Montrealers have witnessed some potent brother acts. The Richards and the Mahovlichs come quickly to mind. Hab fans rate Maurice and Henri Richard as their favourite brother combination on the Habs. Together they accounted for 902 NHL goals.

But it's two brothers who've never come close to scoring a goal who I want to single out now. In the spring of 1971, late in the regular season, fans at the Forum (and I was one of them) were fortunate to witness a unique event in hockey history: two goaltending brothers facing each other across 180 feet of ice. The history makers were Ken and Dave Dryden.

Coincidence brought them to the Forum that night. Ken had been called up from the Nova Scotia Voyageurs late in the season, while Dave had recently moved to Buffalo from Salt Lake City as a backup to Joe Daley. Roger Crozier, the Sabres' number-one man, was suffering from pancreatitis.

We were pumped for the *Hockey Night in Canada* telecast because of the Dryden confrontation. Buffalo coach Punch Imlach did his part to make it a memorable evening by naming Dave Dryden as his starting goalie. But then, to our consternation, Habs coach Al MacNeil listed Rogie Vachon as the Montreal starter. What a spoilsport! Had he no feeling for sports history? This was the same MacNeil who, while coaching Atlanta, would grab Gary Unger by the shirt to prevent him from going on the ice to keep his consecutive-game streak of 914 games alive.

MacNeil would say later, "I started Vachon because I wanted the win and I wanted the two points." This appeared to be a slight to Dryden, who was coming off back-to-back victories, 5–1 over Pittsburgh and 4–1 over Toronto.

The game began and Imlach immediately pulled Dave Dryden and substituted Joe Daley, as if to say, "If MacNeil has no sense of show business, that's his problem."

Halfway through the game, circumstance and coincidence did what MacNeil and Imlach failed to do at the outset. Rogie Vachon lunged for a shot and pulled a groin muscle. Down he went. With Vachon unable to continue, Ken Dryden lumbered off the Montreal bench. That was Imlach's cue to pull Daley and nod at his Dryden: "Get back out there, Dave!"

Thunderous applause greeted the lineup changes as the two lanky netminders pulled on their masks and took their places in goal.

When play resumed, Dave Dryden was the first to falter. With Montreal holding a 2–0 lead, Jacques Lemaire whistled a 70-foot slapper that found the Buffalo net. Montreal now held a 3–0 lead.

Buffalo fought back in the third and scored two goals 48 seconds apart—one by ex-Hab Donnie Marshall, the other by rugged Reg Fleming. But minutes later, Henri Richard faked Dave Dryden out and slipped the puck behind him for Montreal's fourth goal. Guy Lapointe added an empty-netter and the Habs skated off with a 5–2 triumph.

At game's end, the goalies skated slowly to centre ice, shoved their masks high on their heads, grinned at each other, and shook hands. All around them flashbulbs popped as newsmen recorded the moment for posterity.

In the stands, Murray Dryden, the proud father, beamed and told those around him, "I'm glad I came all the way from Toronto to be here tonight. I had a hunch this would happen and I sure didn't want to miss it."

He Turned His Back on the Habs

Most young hockey players would give their right arm to play for the Montreal Canadiens. Well, maybe not their right arm, because they'd need that append-age to help them make the club. But they'd sacrifice a lot, don't you think?

Not Robin Sadler. Remember him? Back in 1975 Robin Sadler was Montreal's top prospect, the Habs' number one draft choice. A mobile defenceman from the Edmonton Oil Kings, he was selected ninth overall and received a $75,000 signing bonus from Sam Pollock.

Before Sadler played a single game in a Montreal uniform, though, he decided that he didn't want to play for the Canadiens after all. He turned his back on pro hockey and returned to his home in Vancouver, where he joined the local fire department. Montrealers shook their heads. How could a top prospect pass up fame and fortune for shift work in a fire hall?

Years later, in 1988, Sadler resurfaced at the Calgary Olympics, where he set the record straight. He hadn't spent the last 13 years fighting fires after all. And he hadn't given up hockey. He'd been playing overseas for more than a decade: a year in Sweden, followed by seasons in Austria, Holland, and then back to Austria. In Calgary he wore the colours of the Austrian national team.

When asked to explain the choices he'd made, he told Bob Mackenzie of the *Hockey News*, "I didn't quit hockey, I just quit pro hockey. And I never became a fireman, I just thought about becoming one.

"I have no regrets, not one. Not playing pro was the best decision I ever made. The one thing I gave up was playing for Montreal, my favourite team. But I had to get out when I did or become a basket case. The European game fit better with what I was looking for."

Doug Jarvis an Overnight Success

When I hosted Montreal Canadiens games on *Hockey Night in Canada* a few years ago, my broadcast partner was Scotty Bowman. We were talking one day about Doug Jarvis and his remarkable 964 consecutive-game streak, an NHL record.

Scotty recalled the beginning of the streak and what a superb faceoff man Jarvis was—right from day one.

"When I was coaching Montreal," Scotty said, "I was talking to Roger Neilson one day. He was coaching the Peterborough juniors at the time and he said to me, 'Scotty, I've got a kid here who's the best faceoff man in hockey. He never loses the draw.' I said, 'Roger, you're talking junior hockey, right?' And he said, 'No, he's the best in all of hockey. I'd stack him up against any centreman in the world.' I said, 'What's the kid's name?' And Roger said, 'Doug Jarvis.'

"The next day I mentioned the name Jarvis to Sam Pollock and Sam snorted, 'No, I'm not interested in the Jarvis kid. He's a small player and our scouts aren't very high on him. But I'll take another look at him if you like.' And Sam did. But he still wasn't impressed and decided not to waste a draft choice on him."

The Leafs, however, did like Jarvis and drafted him in the second round in 1975—24th overall.

Scotty continued, "I still felt that Peter Mahovlich and Jacques Lemaire weren't all that good as faceoff men and I kept bringing Jarvis's name to Sam's attention. I asked Sam if there wasn't some way we could acquire the kid."

Sam told Scotty, "Well, I'm going to be making a deal with the Leafs. They want goalie Wayne Thomas for a first-round draft choice. Maybe the Leafs would like to have Greg Hubick [who'd been playing in Halifax] and I'll ask for Jarvis in return. But I'm sure the Leafs will try to foist Jim McKenny or Brian Glennie or one of their other old guys off on me."

When Sam called Toronto, Jim Gregory, the Leafs' general manager, was out of town. That was a lucky break because Sam got right through to owner Harold Ballard, who fancied he knew as much about hockey as anyone. Sam told Ballard he'd give up Thomas for a draft choice but he still needed a body if the Leafs wanted Hubick. He said to Ballard, "Just give me one of your throwaway players, somebody you're not too high on. But make it a young player, will you? I don't want McKenny or Glennie."

Ballard said, "Well, name somebody. Who do you have in mind?"

Sam replied, "How about that religious kid from Peterborough—Doug Jarvis."

Of course, Sam was aware that Ballard was suspicious of any player who was religious, especially the born-again type. So Ballard, without even consulting Gregory, said, "Okay, Sam, you've got him. It's a deal."

Scotty smiled and said, "So that's how Jarvis came to Montreal. In training camp that year he looked pretty good. Sam kept coming by to ask, 'When are you going to send young Jarvis to Halifax? He's certainly not ready for the NHL.'

"I kept saying, 'Sam, he's holding his own. Let's keep him around for a few more days. I'd like to see what he can do in a preseason game. Well, we went on the road to Chicago and I played Jarvis head-to-head against Stan Mikita, one of the all-time great faceoff men. Jarvis stole the puck from Mikita on almost every faceoff. It was remarkable. I phoned Sam after the game and told him how well Jarvis had played. And Sam said, 'Yeah, yeah, but we should send him down. We can't keep him with the big club. He's simply not ready.'

"Then Jarvis got a big break because Lemaire suffered an injury and couldn't play. I persuaded Sam to keep Jarvis in the lineup for the opening game of the season. He played so well that we couldn't send him down after that. And that was the beginning of his record consecutive-game streak that ended in Hartford a dozen years later at 964 games. Not only that, but he played on a Stanley Cup winner in his rookie season. And for the next three seasons, making it four Cups in his first four years. Incidentally, Greg Hubick, the player Sam gave to Toronto for Jarvis, played a grand total of 77 games in the NHL and scored six goals."

Don Cherry's Long-Standing Nightmare

For as long as he lives, Don Cherry will be hounded by the memory of that steamy night at the Montreal Forum—May 10, 1979—and the seventh game of the Stanley Cup semifinals between the Canadiens and the Boston Bruins.

Cherry's lunchbucket Bruins had scratched and clawed their way to the very brink of dethroning the defending Cup champion Canadiens. The Bruins had won game six in Boston by a 5–2 count and late in game seven they led the Habs 4–3.

It had been 36 years and 13 series since Boston had eliminated the Canadiens in a playoff match-up. Now the drought was almost over. Three minutes left in regulation time. Hab fans who'd marvelled at Gilles Gilbert's tending of the Bruin goal began to despair. They'd all but resigned themselves to the fact it would be Cherry's gritty band of Ratelle, Cashman, Park, Middleton, et al. who'd meet the New York Rangers in the finals. Montreal hopes for a fourth consecutive Cup triumph were slipping away.

Suddenly there was a commotion at the Boston bench. The referee looked over and saw Cherry waving his arms wildly, attempting to call a player back to the gate. Too late. The whistle blew and the Bruins were caught with an extra player on the ice. For the next two minutes, they would have to play shorthanded.

A crescendo of noise filled the Forum as hope was restored. Seconds after play resumed, Jacques Lemaire sped over the Boston line and dropped a pass to Guy Lafleur, and the Flower's shot from a sharp angle found a corner of the Boston goal behind Gilbert. There were 74 seconds left on the clock when the red light flashed.

Earlier in the period, his team trailing 3–1, Lafleur had threaded a perfect pass onto the stick of Mark Napier, who whistled a shot past Gilbert. Napier said later, "If I'd missed that one, I might have ridden the bench for the next five years."

In the overtime, Mario Tremblay drilled a pass across ice to a hustling Yvon Lambert, who took it near the Boston crease and on Montreal's 52nd shot tipped it off Gilbert's pads into the net. Montreal had won 5–4.

Pandemonium, bedlam, frenzy—those were just some of the words used to describe the scene that followed. The Canadiens would advance to the finals, where they would oust the Rangers and win their 22nd Stanley Cup.

The Bruins were dazed and hurt to the quick by the outcome. They could not believe they had come so close to glory only to suffer the shock of bitter defeat. Cherry refused to name the player who'd bolted onto the ice, causing one of the costliest penalties in team history.

Later Cherry would write a book. In it he would say of that moment, "I felt disgusted with myself for letting it happen. Sometimes when you have too many men on the ice it's the player's fault. But not this time. I hadn't spelled out the assignments plainly enough." He added, "A piledriver applied to my stomach could not have created a deeper hurt."

When he boarded the Bruin's charter flight back to Boston that night, Cherry knew he'd coached his last game as a Bruin. Lambert's goal had killed all chances of a return the following season. He went home to face manager Harry Sinden. He went home to be fired.

The Roadrunner Could Fly

He was just a little guy but he had the speed of a lightning bolt, the stamina of a marathon runner, and team spirit in abundance.

Yvan Cournoyer, as a 15-year-old with the Lachine Maroons, was the only francophone on an English-speaking team. When he required a piece of equipment, he would slap the part of his body that needed protection and the trainer would hand over the appropriate item.

Though Cournoyer would soon become bilingual, his real fluency was on the ice. Few could keep pace with him, and when he lengthened his skate blades he took off like a rocket.

He played 14 full seasons and parts of two others with Montreal and might have stayed longer but for a chronic back problem that shortened his career. He competed in 968 NHL games, scoring 428 goals and 435 assists for a career total of 863 points. He lined up with the Habs in a dozen Stanley Cup–playoff years and earned a coveted Stanley Cup ring in ten of them.

In 1972 he was a sparkplug for Team Canada in the Series of the Century against the Soviet Union, even though broadcaster Foster Hewitt could never get his tongue around Yvan's name.

In 15 seasons in Montreal's colours, Cournoyer was the Habs' leading scorer twice and had three seasons when he scored 40 or more goals. He served as team captain from 1975–76 through 1978–79, one of the most glorious eras of Montreal hockey.

A true sportsman, Cournoyer believed in playing by the rules. He accumulated a mere 255 minutes in penalties in his career, an average of less than 17 minutes a season.

His contributions to the game were recognized in 1982 when he was inducted into the Hockey Hall of Fame.

What a Season!

Hockey historian and columnist William Houston, writing in the *Globe and Mail*, concludes that the Montreal Canadiens of 1976–77 were superior to the record-setting Detroit Red Wings of 1995–96. And after watching the '96 Red Wings bow to the Colorado Avalanche in last season's playoffs, I must agree.

Both teams dominated like few others. Coach Scotty Bowman guided Montreal to a 60-8-12 mark in 1976–77. The same man directed the Red Wings to a 62-13-7 record in 1995–96. The Habs of 1976–77 played 80 regular-season games and compiled a winning percentage of .825. The 1995–96 Red Wings played in 82 games for a winning percentage of .799. In 1977 the Canadiens won the Stanley Cup, and nine players from that powerhouse squad are enshrined in the Hockey Hall of Fame, along with general manager Sam Pollock and coach Scotty Bowman.

Bowman's Canadiens outscored his Detroit crew by 62 goals and gave up ten fewer markers. Guy Lafleur (56-80-136) led all NHL scorers in 1976–77 and teammate Steve Shutt (60-45-105) finished third in scoring. Only Sergei Federov (39-68-107) finished among the top ten scorers (tenth) in 1995–96.

The Habs of 1976–77 established several team records, including most wins (60), most road wins (27), fewest losses (8), and fewest home losses (1). Early in the season, Boston edged the Habs 4–3 at the Forum, the lone blemish on Montreal's home record. They played another 34 games at home before losing again.

Montreal, not Detroit, might still hold the record for most wins in a season if games had been decided in overtime during the '70s. Surely they would have won four or five of the dozen that ended in a tie after three periods.

And the '77 Habs produced when it mattered most—in the playoffs. In the Stanley Cup finals, they blanked a strong Boston team in four straight games to duplicate their 4–0 triumph (over Philadelphia) in the '76 finals.

Four in a Row

When the shriek of the siren signalled the end of the 1979 Stanley Cup playoffs, the Canadiens hoisted team captain Bob Gainey to their shoulders. It was Gainey who was judged most valuable of all the Habs as they surged past the New York Rangers in five games and captured their 22nd Stanley Cup.

Gainey contributed six goals and ten assists for 16 playoff points, well in arrears of Jacques Lemaire and Guy Lafleur, who collected 23 points apiece. But Gainey's work ethic and tenacious checking convinced the voters he was the logical choice for MVP and the Conn Smythe Trophy.

Experts had said Montreal's toughest playoff test in '79 would come in the conference final against Don Cherry's Bruins—and they were right. When too many Bruins cluttered the ice in the waning moments of game seven at the Forum, leading to a Montreal comeback and an overtime victory, a fourth consecutive Cup victory was all but assured.

Cherry, who would be reminded of his "too many men" gaffe for the next quarter-century, said of the '79 finals, "Hell, the Rangers were no match for the Canadiens or the Bruins. If we'd won that seventh game in Montreal we would have bounced New York as easily as the Habs did. No question."

When Gainey led his mates around the Forum ice with the Cup, he didn't know it would be another seven years before he would grip base and bowl again. The Islanders and Oilers would dominate the NHL from 1980 to 1990, with four and five Cup wins respectively. Still, the new kids on the block found it hard to overshadow the Habs' domination from 1976 to 1979.

How impressive was Montreal over that span? Famed broadcaster Dick Irvin considers those Montreal championship teams to be the best ever assembled. And he may be right.

No team since has matched Montreal's regular-season records for those four seasons:

Season	W	L	T
1975–76	58	11	11
1976–77	60	8	12
1977–78	59	10	11
1978–79	52	17	11

At playoff time over that span, the Habs were almost invincible. In 1976 they won the Stanley Cup in 13 playoff games, losing only one game. In 1977 they won 12 games, losing twice. In 1978 the Habs won 12 games and lost three, and in 1979 they retained the Cup with a 12 and 4 record. From 1976 through 1979 their playoff record was 48 and 10.

A record-tying fifth consecutive Stanley Cup triumph became a near impossibility for a number of reasons: a) Ken Dryden retired; b) Scotty Bowman resigned to take over as coach and GM in Buffalo; c) Jacques Lemaire left the team to play in Switzerland; and d) Yvan Cournoyer's aching back forced him to retire.

Six Cup Wins for Dryden

Ken Dryden played on six Stanley Cup–winning teams with the Canadiens but only the last Cup was won at the Forum; the rest were all won on the road. Dryden recalls winning the trophy in Chicago in 1971, after a seven-game series with the Blackhawks, and remembers feeling at the time that a road win was rather nice.

"You have the Cup all to yourself for a few hours, you enjoy the celebration in the dressing room. There's the bus trip to the airport with the Cup on board and the charter flight back to Montreal. By then we were ready to share our triumph with the thousands of fans who were at the airport to greet us in the early morning hours."

In 1979, Dryden's final season, Montreal won the Cup on home ice against the Rangers. He knew that he would retire that year, and he remembers the last fifteen seconds of the championship game, with the Habs about to clinch the victory.

"There was a faceoff outside the Montreal zone and a few seconds later Eddie Johnstone of the Rangers fired the puck in along the boards. It squirted in behind my net and I moved quickly to trap it there. That's when I heard the final buzzer. The crowd was roaring and I stood there with the puck in my hand—a lovely souvenir of a special occasion.

"Then Matt Pavelich, one of the game officials, was at my side, saying, 'Kenny, can I have the puck? Can I have the puck? This is my final game as a linesman.'

"I said, 'Matt, it's my last game too. I'd like to keep the puck.'

"But when I looked at him and saw in his eyes how important that puck was to him, and when I thought of how many more years he'd been around than I, I turned my glove over and dropped the puck into his hand."

Dryden's career with the Habs covered only eight seasons, from 1970 to 1979. He sat out the 1973–74 campaign to article for a Toronto law firm and to protest his low salary as a Canadien. He won 258 games, lost only 57, and tied 74. His goals-against average was 2.24. He won 80 of 112 playoff games for Montreal, captured or shared the Vezina Trophy five times, and is the only NHL goalie to record over 200 wins and achieve a winning percentage of more than .700.

The Cup Goes Missing

On May 21, 1979, the Montreal Canadiens joyously celebrated their fourth consecutive Stanley Cup victory. While the players were toasting their triumph at Henri Richard's tavern, Guy Lafleur slipped away from his mates, grabbed the Stanley Cup without being spotted, and deposited it in the trunk of his car. Nobody noticed that the Cup left when Lafleur did.

Lafleur drove to Thurso, Quebec, and the home of his parents. There he proudly placed the gleaming trophy on the front lawn and invited the folks in the neighbourhood to come and see it. People came from miles around once the news spread. Flashbulbs popped as close friends, relatives, and complete strangers posed beside hockey's most prized possession.

In Montreal, meanwhile, a frantic search was being organized. The Stanley Cup was missing. Who could have stolen it? Lafleur's name wasn't even on the list of suspects.

Later that day, in Thurso, Guy Lafleur's conscience began to bother him. Perhaps his theft of the Cup wasn't such a brilliant idea after all, even though it seemed to please everyone in town. When Guy looked out the front window and saw his son Martin filling the Cup with water from the garden hose, he knew it was time to retrieve the priceless trophy, dry it off, and get it back to the Montreal Forum.

That's where he deposited it a few hours later. The men responsible for the Cup's safety were annoyed with Guy, saying his little prank wasn't funny and wasn't appreciated. They grumbled on, but who among them would dare chastise the man who'd just led the Canadiens to the Stanley Cup with his ten goals and 23 points?

A Dynasty Crumbles

The Montreal Canadiens were still celebrating their fourth straight Stanley Cup triumph in 1979 when they began to think ahead to the following season. Only one NHL team had captured five consecutive Cups—the Habs of 1956–60. It would be a sparkling jewel in their crown if the 1979–80 Canadiens could match the winning streak of their famous brethren from the '50s.

But suddenly large cracks began to appear in the assembly of solid hockey talent. The Habs had won the '79 Cup without the guiding hand of Sam Pollock, who had departed the summer before. Now, in the postseason, Al MacNeil, supervisor of the Nova Scotia operation, a vital artery to the big club, announced he was leaving to become coach of the Atlanta Flames.

One week before the entry draft, there was a bigger bombshell. Scotty Bowman revealed that he was departing Montreal to become coach and general manager of the Buffalo Sabres. Bowman had been deeply wounded when he was bypassed as Pollock's successor, and had been seeking greener pastures. Pollock's replacement, the inexperienced Irving Grundman, was said to be taking too many bows for Montreal's success. Montrealers felt that Bowman, a native son, fluently bilingual, was destined to be a fixture around the Forum for the rest of his hockey life. It was a real shock when he waved good-bye and shuffled off to Buffalo.

Then, incredibly, Jacques Lemaire followed Bowman out the door. Lemaire, 33, with three or four more good seasons in front of him, signed with a team in Switzerland as a player-coach. And he was just the first player to leave. Other Habs took flight, almost as if the Montreal dressing room was a crime scene and they were the prime suspects.

The next hero to slip away was Ken Dryden, 32, who announced he was ready to pursue challenges other than hockey. Dryden had earned his law degree and was regarded as a man of great intellect, a multitalented individual to whom life was more than blocking hockey pucks and savouring the crowd's applause. Goaltending was merely a slice of life. Now it was time to see what other tasty slices lay ahead.

Dryden, whose unique writing skills would soon be tapped, had been on six Cup winners in eight years, had been a key performer for Team Canada '72, had won numerous awards and All-Star berths, and that appeared to be more than enough for the scholarly netminder.

Another gaping hole on the roster was created when Yvan Cournoyer departed. The Roadrunner's chronic back problems forced him to turn in his jersey in training camp. Sadly, there hasn't been a "beep-beep" player of his calibre, one with speed and flair and a knack for scoring spectacular goals, to come along and have us declare, "There he is, another Yvan!" When he turned in his sticks—all as short as an old man's cane—and walked away, the Habs lost a game little man with an abundance of talent.

Many people were further shocked when Grundman announced the signing of "Boom Boom" Geoffrion as the new head coach of the Habs. In his book *Robinson for the Defence*, Larry Robinson noted that Geoffrion had coached twice before, for the Rangers and the Flames. "Both times he'd quit because of the pressures of the job; this time he'd plunged headlong into the most intense pressure-cooker in the sport!" It was clear to Robinson and his mates that Geoffrion had problems from the beginning. "He knew what he wanted us to do but he just couldn't get his message across to the players," said Robinson.

Geoffrion had some difficult acts to follow. He was funnier than his predecessors and he could sing better. He was good in commercials on TV. But he couldn't run a team like Blake and Bowman. Traditionally, the Habs were told to "Play the way I tell you to play. If not, you won't be around very long." Geoffrion had played for Blake and knew what dedication and discipline meant. As the new coach, he expected commitment but he didn't demand it. And he didn't get it. The players began questioning his approach, his game plan. Some gave him less than 100 percent. Those who did give him total effort—Robinson and Gainey among them—lost confidence in his ability to lead. Early in the season Gainey and Geoffrion had some heated arguments over a variety of coaching decisions. The players, as you can imagine, sided with Gainey. Thirty games into the season, Geoffrion threw up his arms and resigned.

He was replaced by Claude Ruel, who brought some harmony to the club. Despite their problems, the Habs finished in third place overall with 107 points (behind Philadelphia with 116 points and Buffalo with 110). They entered the playoffs riding a 22-game undefeated streak.

But Ruel, who relied far too often on his veterans and ignored his young players, guided a club into the postseason that was reeling with exhaustion. Injuries piled up—to Lafleur and Larouche (100 goals between them), to Savard and Lapointe. The roster was decimated, the survivors too weak to topple Minnesota in the quarterfinals. Hopes of five Stanley Cups in a row were dashed when Minnesota ousted the Habs in seven games.

At the end of the season, Ruel resigned.

Habs' Biggest Draft Blunder

It may have seemed like a logical draft choice at the time, the time being June of 1980. After all, Doug Wickenheiser of Regina had a reputation as a big, tough centreman, a graduating junior player with immense potential. Montrealers thought hometown favourite Denis Savard, not as big as Wickenheiser, perhaps not as tough, but built along the lines of Henri Richard, could do everything the Regina boy could do at centre ice, and perhaps many things more. That may be, argued the Montreal scouts, but teams in the '80s covet size, muscle, and strength in their recruits. There's going to be less room in future for the good little man. So the Canadiens, with first choice, selected Wickenheiser.

The Chicago Blackhawks, unable to believe that the Habs had passed up a chance to snare a French-Canadian phenom, a young man who already resembled the Pocket Rocket, a teenager who had become the idol of the Quebec junior crowds, grabbed Savard with their first choice—and without a moment's hesitation. (Winnipeg drafted second, and, like Montreal, opted for size and strength. The Jets chose defenceman David Babych.)

Savard blossomed almost immediately in Chicago and averaged slightly more than 100 points per season in a decade of play there. Wickenheiser struggled from the moment he donned a Montreal jersey. After months of mediocrity, when stardom appeared to be beyond his reach, he was dealt to the St. Louis Blues for Perry Turnbull. After half a season—and seven goals—Turnbull was traded to Winnipeg for Lucien Deblois, who stayed for a cup of coffee and moved on to the Leafs.

Irving Grundman, manager of the Habs in 1980, has borne the brunt of the criticism for the Wickenheiser fiasco. It's one of the decisions that cost him his job. How often he must say, "If only I'd chosen Savard, or, if not him, Paul Coffey, who was the sixth junior taken in 1980..."

But the tantalizing vision of Denis Savard in Montreal colours stayed in the minds of his successors, even when injuries slowed him down and his numbers began to decline. In 1990, when the Blackhawks signalled they were ready to deal, the Habs willingly parted with defenceman Chris Chelios, a Norris Trophy winner the previous season, in order to get Savard. They even tossed in a second-round draft choice to sweeten the pot.

Savard averaged 25 goals per season with his new team but his age was showing. There'd be no more 100-point seasons. In 1993 he was signed as a free agent by Tampa Bay and in 1995 he returned to Chicago.

Chelios, meanwhile, has been a perennial all-star in Chicago, one of the highest-scoring, toughest defencemen in the NHL.

Hockey commentator Don Cherry was appalled when he heard of the 1990 trade. He told columnist Jim Proudfoot of the *Toronto Star*, "If Chelios' name had been Tremblay, the trade would never have been made. Chelios is tough as nails. At his best in the clutch. And a couple of years younger than Savard. Montreal was thinkin' Savard and Stephane Richer would form a dynamite combination. But they didn't fit together because both of them want the puck a lot of the time. There was no fit. And they also figured their young defensemen would get better and replace Chelios. Has that happened? Holy geez, givin' up Chelios. Now that's hard to believe."

Fergie Victim of Savard's Devilish Humour

John Ferguson teed up his golf ball and stepped back a few feet. I had made him smile a moment earlier by asking him to relate the story of an incident going back to 1972. Now I wanted to hear about it firsthand. Fergie leaned on his driver and told me how Serge Savard had suckered him almost a quarter of a century earlier.

"Right after Team Canada beat the Soviets in 1972, I went around the dressing room in Moscow and had the players sign a special hockey stick for me. I really treasured that stick and planned to have it mounted in my den when I got home. Well, you'll recall the huge welcome-home reception we got when we arrived back in Canada. Prime Minister Trudeau was there to greet us and I followed Serge Savard through the reception line, still clutching my hockey stick. Trudeau shook hands with Savard and I couldn't believe my ears when I heard Serge say to him, 'By the way, Mr. Prime Minister, look what John Ferguson has brought you from Moscow—an autographed hockey stick.'

"Son of a bitch! Savard took the stick from my hands and placed it in Trudeau's. I was speechless. I wanted to throttle Savard. Trudeau thanked me and suddenly my prize was gone, handed over to Trudeau, and then passed along to one of his flunkeys."

"You never got it back?" I asked.

"Nah. Someone from Trudeau's office called me one day. I guess he'd heard about the joke Savard had concocted. He asked if I wanted the stick back and I said I guessed not. I said Trudeau could keep it."

"He should have sent it back no matter what you said," I told him. "That stick meant a lot more to you than it ever did to Trudeau."

Fergie shrugged.

Note to Pierre Elliott Trudeau:

Pierre, if you ever read this book, why not find that stick and send it back to John Ferguson?

Dick Irvin Recalls the Unknown Goaltender

My friendship with Dick Irvin goes back a long way. Oldtimers around Montreal may recall that we worked together on CFCF-TV when it first went on the air in Montreal in the early '60s. A few years ago Dick wrote a fine book, *The Habs*, in which he describes the most emotional and dramatic event he's covered in more than a quarter-century of broadcasting Montreal games.

Dick says, "It was a playoff series that had everything, an underdog team eliminating the best team in hockey in the first round; an unknown goaltender with six games of NHL experience winning the Conn Smythe Trophy as the playoff MVP; a revered French-Canadian hockey hero publicly criticizing his English-speaking coach, igniting a front-page media war with severe linguistic overtones. Then, as the final curtain fell, one of the Montreal Canadiens' all-time greatest superstars was carrying the Stanley Cup off the ice at the Chicago Stadium, his final act in what had been the final game of a now legendary career."

Halfway through Dick's summation, any Montreal fan worth his salt realized the esteemed commentator was talking about the 1971 playoffs and a stunning triumph for the Montreal Canadiens.

The underdog team was Montreal, of course, called on to face the mighty Boston Bruins of Orr, Esposito, Cashman, Bucyk, and others in the first round of the playoffs. The Bruins had won the Stanley Cup the previous season and they would capture it again in 1972. Their 1971 squad was perhaps the strongest of the three finalists, evidenced by their margin over the Habs at the end of the 1970–71 regular season: 24 points.

Perhaps the Bruins took the Habs too lightly that spring. After all, the Bruins were the defending champions and the Canadiens hadn't even made the playoffs the previous season (even though they'd accumulated 92 points, the highest point total ever for a non-playoff team).

And the Bruins were facing a rookie netminder with six games' experience under his chest protector, a tall, studious-looking, ex-college player with poor eyesight. His name was Dryden—Ken Dryden.

Veteran Johnny Bucyk, who played 21 of his 23 NHL seasons with Boston, recalls approaching that series with confidence, even though, over two decades, none of the Boston teams he'd played on had won even a single series against the Habs.

"It was Dryden who beat us in '71," he says, looking back. "I know we had the better team but Dryden got hot and beat us."

Boston superstar Phil Esposito complained that Dryden made saves that were out of this world. "The guy has arms like a giraffe," Phil testified, and when it was pointed out that giraffes were more noted for their elongated necks than their long arms, he shrugged and said, "Ah, you know what I mean. So we never had a zoo in Sault Ste. Marie, where I grew up."

Boston goalie Gerry Cheevers, who was keeping notes in his diary at that time for a book called *Goaltender*, wrote that "Dryden, the budding lawyer, appears to have awfully fast hands. We've seen him under fire now and I guess he'll be around for awhile. For one so young he has remarkable composure. And he has the best left hand I've seen since Jacques Plante's."

Cheevers and the Bruins almost lost Bobby Orr in game one at Boston. Orr was livid when he drew a penalty and growled something at referee John Ashley, who added ten minutes to Orr's time in the box. Orr then leaped from the box ("You'd have thought somebody had lanced his ass with a six-inch needle," wrote Cheevers) and tried to get at Ashley. But the linesmen intercepted Orr and three or four Bruins herded him to the dressing room, saving him from a game misconduct and a suspension.

Cheevers, Esposito, Bucyk, and the rest of the Bruins would later agree that game two was the turning point in the series. After Boston captured game one 3–1 in front of Cheevers, Boston coach Tom Johnson switched to goalie Eddie Johnston (the second-guessers said it was a big mistake) for game two. The Bruins flew into a 5–1 lead. Then Beliveau, in his final season, rallied the Habs as he had done so often in the past. Late in the second period, Henri Richard scored and there was hope. Montreal lit up the third period with five straight goals to win 7–5. Dryden made so many incredible saves that Esposito finally stood next to him, staring at him. Then he skated away, shaking his head in disbelief and frustration.

Backup goalie Cheevers figured Beliveau and Richard, 74 years between them, acted like there was some kind of law against anybody else winning but Montreal. "Those Frenchmen go slightly glassy-eyed when they get thinking of their tradition and their pride and all the rest of that bullshit," he said. "Then they suddenly acquire adrenalin not available to other teams."

Cheevers displayed his edginess when the series switched to Montreal. A young boy holding a dog on a leash taunted him outside the Boston team bus. "Hey Cheevers," he said, "We beat you Bruins tomorrow." Cheevers snarled back, "Shut up, kid, or I'll cut the balls off your dog."

On the Forum ice, the Canadiens won again, 3–1. Dryden made a save off Esposito that drew the ultimate compliment from the Boston sniper. "It was the greatest save anybody made off me," said Espo. "The best one ever."

Dryden, down on his knees, followed the puck across the crease to his right. Just then, Cashman flipped the puck over to Esposito standing in front of the net and Espo saw four or five feet of open net. He whipped the puck into the hole and it disappeared—right into Dryden's glove. Superman couldn't have reacted any faster. Cheevers called it "an amazing feat of dexterity."

The Bruins won game four 5–2 and rained rubber at Dryden in game five—23 shots in the first period, 12 in the second, and 21 more in the third—and coasted to a 7–3 victory. But Dryden bounced back with another solid effort in game six and the Habs rolled to a surprise 8–3 win to tie the series at three games apiece.

Dryden's composure throughout the series worried Cheevers. He noticed that the rookie, between flurries around his net, rested on one foot and placed the point of his goal stick on the ice. Then he rested his chin on his gloves at the knob of the stick, as relaxed as a guy watching a ballet. Cheevers would remark, "Dryden picked one hell of a time to play the best goal of his life. The long-legged son of a bitch was robbing us of a lot of goals—and a lot of money."

The Canadiens went on to eliminate the Bruins, a team that set 37 team records during the regular season, with a 4–2 triumph in game seven. It was a huge playoff upset. Cheevers was tempted to join the lineup of players shaking hands when it was over. He wanted to tell Dryden, the big giraffe, that he'd done a masterful job. But Cheevers said to hell with it. He'd never congratulated anyone in the past for taking money out of his pockets and he wasn't about to change his style. Instead, back in the Bruin dressing room, he took Jacques Beauchamp, a Montreal reporter, aside and said, "Jacques, you tell that kid he had a hell of a series. Give him my best."

The Second-Best Brother Combination

By the time Frank Mahovlich joined the Habs in 1971, he had won four Stanley Cups as a Leaf and played with Gordie Howe and Alex Delvecchio in Detroit, where he scored a career-high 49 goals. His brother Pete, a gifted centre, was a Detroit teammate until he was dealt to Montreal in 1969.

The Habs wanted the elder Mahovlich as well and on January 13, 1971, they willingly traded Mickey Redmond, Guy Charron, and Bill Collins to the Wings in order to get him. Frank responded by leading the Habs to the 1971 Stanley Cup with a record 14 playoff goals. The Big M tallied 96 and 93 points in his first two seasons in Montreal and played on another Cup winner in 1973. He scored 31 goals in his final season at the Forum and lifted his career totals to 533 goals and 1,103 points. His kid brother, meanwhile, excelled at centre and proved to be an outstanding checker and penalty killer. Pete gained worldwide fame with a spectacular goal against Soviet netminder Vladislav Tretiak in game two of the 1972 series at Maple Leaf Gardens in Toronto.

As a brother combination, they were never as popular as the Richards. How could they be? But they were good. They were very good, good enough for both to be selected for Team Canada in '72. Frank left the Habs first, unable to refuse a huge salary offered by the Toronto Toros of the WHA in 1974. Three seasons later, Pete was traded to Pittsburgh.

NBC Anticipates Great Goaltending Duel

In May 1973 I teamed up with fellow announcers Ted Lindsay and Tim Ryan for a playoff game between the Canadiens and the Chicago Blackhawks at the Montreal Forum. It was game five of the finals and it matched two of the greatest goaltenders of the era, Tony Esposito and Ken Dryden. Dryden and Esposito were the focus of all the hype that NBC lavished on the event.

On the eve of the game, Tim, Ted, and I were sharing a bottle of wine in a Montreal bistro, when Tim looked over to the bar where Esposito and Gary Smith, Chicago's backup netminder, were nursing a couple of beers.

It grew late, midnight came and went, and Tim asked, "Don't the Blackhawks have a curfew? Why are those guys still there?" Another half-hour passed and Tim said, "I can't take this." He walked up to the bar and told the two goalies, "Hey, one of you guys had better go to bed. You're play-ing the biggest game of your season tomorrow on national TV." They just laughed. The next day, the great goaltending battle we'd expected fizzled out in the early moments of play. First one team scored, then the other. And it went that way for the full sixty minutes. Chicago won the game 8–7 and the teams established a playoff record for the most goals in a game in a final series: 15. The goaltending at both ends was dreadful.

"Geez," Tim said, after the debacle. "We all knew where Tony was last night. I wonder what the hell Dryden was doing?"

Montreal captured the next game and won the series four games to two.

Other Superstars of the '70s

Great success was achieved by the Habs in the '70s because of the blend of talent on the team. While Guy Lafleur was hailed for being the top offensive player on the club, Bob Gainey was recognized for being the premier defensive specialist. Gainey's splendid two-way play earned him accolades from the Soviet coaches and earned him the first four Frank J. Selke Awards ever presented.

In 1973 most Hab fans were astonished when the Canadiens "gambled" a first-round draft choice on a Peterborough kid who had struggled to score 20 goals in junior hockey while others around him were scoring three times that number. At the time, Scotty Bowman had a number of prolific scorers. He needed a player who could check. Gainey proved to be outstanding in a defensive role, sacrificing personal glory and providing leadership that later earned him the captain's "C"—which he held for eight seasons. Gainey played on five Cup winners, won the Conn Smythe Trophy in 1979, and collected 239 goals (not bad for a chap who had trouble finding the net). After retiring as a player, Gainey has been acclaimed as a coach and general manager in the NHL and recently signed a new three-year contract with the Dallas Stars.

Larry Robinson loved athletics from the day he learned to skate by pushing a chair around the ice in his home town of Marvellville, Ontario. One day the chair slipped away from him, but he didn't fall on his face—he skated!

He was a superb high-school athlete, excelling in track and field events and in football. Some of his high-school records have never been broken. One year his football team went undefeated, scored 200 points without having a point scored against it.

In hockey, as an eight-year-old he was playing against teenagers.

He played his junior A hockey in Kitchener and was part of an unusual draft in 1971. Sam Pollock had managed to snare four top draft choices that year and named Guy Lafleur (1), Chuck Arnason (7), Murray Wilson (11), and Larry Robinson (20). Larry was both stunned and disappointed when he heard his name called. He was newly married, needed money, and figured it would be years before he'd be good enough to crack the Montreal lineup. After a year and a half in the minors in Halifax, Larry was called up in January 1973 and adjusted rapidly to the fast pace of the NHL.

In the 1973 playoffs, he scored a goal he'll never forget. Against Philadelphia in game two in the second round, Larry led a rush up-ice in sudden-death overtime. He was nervous and wanted to pass the puck but Frank Mahovlich, skating alongside, yelled at him, "Go with it!" Larry obeyed his elder and drilled a shot from the blue line that sailed into the Philadelphia net. He'd scored his first playoff goal, a game winner. That goal, which boosted his confidence, was a turning point.

He went on to a brilliant career, played 17 seasons with Montreal and three more with Los Angeles. He won six Stanley Cups as a player and one as an assistant coach with New Jersey. He holds the NHL record for most playoff games by a defenceman (227) and most consecutive years in the playoffs (20). He captured the Norris Trophy twice and the Conn Smythe Trophy as playoff MVP in 1978.

Accompanying Robinson on defence for a number of years were two other outstanding defencemen, Serge Savard and Guy Lapointe. All three made it to the Hockey Hall of Fame—and deservedly so. Savard captained the Canadiens from 1979 to 1981, played on eight Stanley Cup–winning teams, and captured the Conn Smythe Trophy in 1969. Robinson once said of Savard, "He was our E. F. Hutton. He didn't talk much but when he did open up, everyone listened." Savard was appointed managing director of the Habs in 1983, and under his direction Montreal won the Stanley Cup in 1986 and again in 1993. Many fans were shocked and saddened when Savard was unceremoniously dismissed from his position early in the 1995–96 season. They figured severing all ties with such a hockey legend was a departure from the Canadiens' classy style.

Guy Lapointe was a marvellous defender for the Habs during the '70s, a Montreal East Ender who was renowned for his practical jokes and his seemingly effortless style. I asked him once, "Is it true you collected the players' dentures on a road trip and mailed them back to the Forum?" He grinned slyly and said, "Oh, no. Not me." Lapointe, Robinson, and Savard became known as the "Big Three," although Savard disliked the description, pointing out time after time that the team was much more than three defencemen. There were nights when Lapointe could play like Bobby Orr; well, almost like Orr. In his final few seasons with the Habs, Lapointe ran into several injuries, agonized over a painful divorce, and bickered with coach Claude Ruel. At age 34 he was traded to St. Louis. But he's remembered fondly.

Steve Shutt could make any defenceman look bad. He'd pop in and out of the slot, ready to pounce on a loose puck and deliver a lightning-fast shot on the net. Larry Robinson said Shutt had the fastest hands he'd ever seen on a player—faster than Mike Bossy's. Shutt scored 424 career goals, most of them as a Hab left winger, and shares the club record of 60 goals in a season with Guy Lafleur. He's also a five-time winner of the Stanley Cup.

In the late '70s, ten years after he broke in with the Canadiens, Jacques "Coco" Lemaire was one of the best centres in hockey. He had great speed and a wicked shot. He could pass the puck with uncanny accuracy—and hard. He tried to avoid the limelight and the backslappers that surround every successful team. And he was a student of the game. When he'd had enough, after the 1979 Stanley Cup victory party, he signed to play and coach in Switzerland. But it wasn't long before he was back in the NHL, coaching the Habs. And in 1995 he coached the underdog New Jersey Devils—with Larry Robinson at his side—to the Stanley Cup.

Chapter 7
COREY AND RECENT CONFLICTS

Corey at the Top

There is a famous book, *The Hockey Sweater* by Roch Carrier, in which all the children in a small French community idolize Rocket Richard. They all wear number 9 on their hockey sweaters like Maurice Richard, they tape their sticks like Maurice Richard, they even dab Vaseline on their hair like Maurice Richard. Naturally, they all want to grow up to be hockey stars like Maurice Richard.

Such a boy was Ronald Corey, who, growing up in Montreal's East End, said daily prayers for Maurice Richard. The memories of watching the Rocket play at the Forum—Corey managed about two trips a season—will last him a lifetime.

As a youth Corey wore number 9 on his back. In time he caught the eye of a Canadiens scout and was invited to a junior training camp in Verdun, a two and a half hour tram ride from his home. He was 16 years old.

Joining him there was another teenage prospect, Claude Ruel, and Corey remembers being amazed at how fast Ruel could skate. "As for me, they told me I couldn't skate, not fast enough, anyway, and they sent me home after the fourth day. It was the end for me. The end came for Ruel three seasons later when he lost an eye playing hockey."

Corey studied journalism and became a hockey reporter. He ran a muffler company, was head of marketing for a brewery, and, in time, became a TV producer at Radio Canada. I met him many times when he was in TV sports and remember thinking he'd found his niche in life. Apparently he didn't agree. Ambition propelled him upward. New challenges intrigued him.

In 1982 he was offered a position he never dreamed would be his: president of *Le Club de Hockey Canadien, Inc.* He has survived 15 years of triumph and turmoil and celebrated two Stanley Cup victories, in 1986 and 1993.

His first major test came after a few months on the job. Irv Grundman, who had succeeded Sam Pollock as general manager, was floundering. He'd won a Stanley Cup in his first year in charge—with Pollock's disciples still around—but he'd had problems ever since. The Habs had won just one playoff series in four years. Grundman's critics blamed him for a disastrous trade, sending Rod Langway, Craig Laughlin, Brian Engblom, and Doug Jarvis to Washington for defenceman Rick Green and forward Ryan Walter. It was Grundman, they said, who failed to keep Ken Dryden and Jacques Lemaire happy, who drove Scotty Bowman out of town (to Buffalo), and who failed to inform Bob Berry, his coach, of the deals he was concocting.

Corey vowed to learn from these events. When drastic action was called for, Corey delivered. "Because the club had gone nowhere in the playoffs," he told reporters. "I had to make a move—a drastic move."

Corey fired Grundman in 1983, shortly after the Habs lost a best-of-five playoff series to Bowman's Buffalo Sabres. Corey then dismissed Ron Caron, director of personnel and recruitment. Irving Grundman's son Howard resigned as director of hockey operations. Bob Berry, the unpopular coach, was relieved of his duties and offered a job as a scout.

To replace Grundman, Corey signed Serge Savard, who, as a player, always had the right answers. That's how he earned the nickname "Senator." Savard surprised everyone by retaining Berry as coach, even though Berry had infuriated 99 percent of the media and most of his players. Wrong answer, Serge. Recognizing his mistake midway through the 1983–84 season, Savard fired Berry. Guy Carbonneau said of Berry's dismissal, "We were all sick of Bob Berry." Larry Robinson analysed Berry and said Berry was intimidated by the fish bowl that is Montreal hockey. Robinson added two more complaints. Berry coached man-to-man hockey, a style that is outdated and doesn't work in today's game, and his practices were always the same—boring.

Savard persuaded Berry's assistant coach, former teammate Jacques Lemaire, to come on board. Outspoken winger Steve Shutt said of Lemaire, "There's no way he's ready to coach here. There's too much pressure." Shutt was wrong. Lemaire was an immediate success, probably because he dumped the man-on-man system and made the practices more stimulating. He proved to be a very shrewd coach.

Through all of these moves, Corey remained a concerned observer and contributor of ideas and opinions. He was developing a reputation as a leader who did not procrastinate, a man who wielded authority always with the interests of the team's success in mind. If coaching careers went crashing, if superstars were traded, so be it. If Corey didn't make the tough decisions, his own career, his qualifications to be the man at the top, would be questioned by powerful men above the top. It's an old saying but it contains some truth: everybody has a boss.

Corey Cleans House

It was a stunning announcement. Four games into the 1995–96 season, on Tuesday, October 17, 1995, Canadiens president Ronald Corey called a press conference at the Forum to reveal that his team no longer had a general manager, an assistant general manager, or even a coach. Three hours earlier he'd dismissed Serge Savard, who'd been general manager of the Habs since April 1983, Savard's assistant, Andre Boudrias, and coach Jacques Demers, who was beginning his fourth season behind the Montreal bench.

Corey's actions left the hockey world in shock. The firings were a complete surprise to Savard and Demers. Savard left the club immediately, while Demers was offered another position within the organization.

The media, hastily assembled to record Corey's explanation for his startling decision, were further amazed when he confessed he had nobody in mind to fill the vacancies.

"I'll get right to it," he said. "It's important that we get the right people."

A dozen names surfaced immediately. John Ferguson ("Not interested"), Pat Burns ("Molson's couldn't sell enough beer to get me back to Montreal"), Fredericton coach Paulin Bordeleau, Anaheim assistant GM Pierre Gauthier, Islanders assistant Guy Charron, and Ottawa assistant Alain Vignault were among the candidates rumoured to be on Corey's list.

Four days later Corey had his new employees in place and introduced them at another press conference prior to the Habs' next home game, a clash with the Toronto Maple Leafs.

More surprises!

From the public-relations department at Molson's came Rejean Houle, the new general manager—counted on to fill Savard's big shoes. Houle, it was noted, had never held a position besides that of player, with any NHL club. Mario Tremblay, a former Hab winger, was plucked from the broadcast booth to replace Demers as coach. Tremblay's coaching experience: none. "But I've played for some great coaches," Mario was quick to point out. Yvan Cournoyer was named as an assistant coach. His only coaching experience came from guiding his roller hockey team to the league finals in 1995.

Hockey commentator and writer Bob Mackenzie said, "The tandem of ex-Hab Houle and ex-Hab Tremblay is long on tradition, heavy on heart and character, but devoid of anything approximating managerial or coaching experience. The odds of this duo being wildly successful with on-the-job training have to be stacked against them."

Jim Hunt, another veteran hockey observer, said on radio that he recalled Houle from 1974 "as a bit of an airhead." He added, "His job at Molson's was counting the empties for that's what PR people do." Hunt noted that Tremblay, "the Don Cherry of French-language TV," had never coached hockey before, and reminded listeners about the Leafs' performance under Mike Nykoluk, a previous broadcaster turned coach. Hunt concluded, "I doubt if the Habs will win ten games all season."

Mackenzie was upset when the Habs severed their longtime relationship with Savard. He noted that Corey was within his rights, "although the severing of all ties with a Hab legend of Savard's stature ranks as almost unforgivable." He suggested Corey's moves "reek of panic" and when "Houle went on about the 20 Stanley Cups the new group has between them he neglected to mention the 10 that went out the door with Savard."

The three newcomers—all very popular and all francophones—proved during their first day on the job that lack of experience wasn't a factor. Playing against the Leafs that night, the Habs came through with a last-second 3–2 victory, a result that prompted the emotional Tremblay to high-five his players and his new boss, Ronald Corey.

A follow-up lopsided 6–2 win over the previously undefeated Los Angeles Kings silenced the critics of the shake-up, at least temporarily.

Corey's retooling of the Canadiens had been done boldly and confidently. He had one more major decision to make: what to do with fan favourite Patrick Roy? It was a decision made easier when Roy himself unexpectedly provided the perfect excuse for a trade.

On December 2, 1995, there was an amazing eruption of emotion at the Forum. It was a public confrontation between goaltender Patrick Roy and the Habs' new coach, Mario Tremblay, a clash of wills that was witnessed by millions on *Hockey Night in Canada*.

On the ice, the Canadiens were blown away by Detroit 11–1, and Roy was furious at his new coach for not yanking him from the match when it was obvious he was having a terrible game. Roy didn't get the hook until he'd allowed nine of the goals. As he skated to the Montreal bench, totally humiliated, Roy brushed by Tremblay, then turned and elbowed his way past him again. Roy decided that what he had to say would be aimed at team president Ron Corey, seated a few feet away.

"That's the last time I'll play for Montreal," the veteran puckstopper vowed.

If Roy expected to win Corey's sympathy in his dispute with Tremblay, he didn't get it. Nor should he have expected it. Knowing Corey as well as he did, Roy should have known that the team president would throw his full support behind his new management team. The moment Patrick Roy uttered those hot words at the Forum, his career as a Canadien was over. Four days later Roy and Mike Keane were traded to Colorado in return for Jocelyn Thibault, Martin Rucinsky, and Andrei Kovalenko. Houle made the deal under pressure and in haste. But he emerged from it smelling of roses. Thibault played in 40 games, compiling a 23-13-3 mark, compared to Roy's 39-game Colorado record of 22-15-1. Keane scored a mere ten goals with the Avalanche and was the only player on the roster in the minus category (−5). Rucinsky (29-46-75) and Kovalenko (28-28-56) had career seasons with the Habs.

The first time Roy faced his old mates in a game was on February 5, 1996, in Colorado. Roy played brilliantly, making 37 saves in a 4–2 Avalanche victory. Handed the puck at the end of the game, Roy flipped the disc at Tremblay as his former coach walked across the ice. In a post-game interview, Roy said, "That was for the fans. I think they love it as much as me. Every athlete has got pride and I wanted to show my new fans I could give them good hockey. I wanted to show that Montreal made a mistake."

A tight-lipped Tremblay said, "I'm really disappointed in what happened. But he did it and he has to live with it. He's a great goalie who played a great game and I don't want to talk about it."

Montreal defenceman Lyle Odelein was less forgiving. He said, "What Patrick did was brutal. The guy played a great game but at the end he was playing to the crowd...making easy shots look hard. Why didn't he leave it at that? Now everybody's talking about what he did at the end."

Roy admitted his actions were arrogant but all part of his personality. He even admitted he'd promised his Colorado mates a $3,000 party if they won the game that night against the Habs.

By season's end, those who had predicted a disastrous future for the Habs without "St. Patrick," those who had ridiculed Corey's appointments, the scoffers who had openly sneered at his coaching staff's credentials, were absolutely mute. They grudgingly admitted that things had turned out rather well after all. For the Habs had rolled their way to a respectable 40 wins and 90 points, good enough for sixth place overall in the Eastern Conference standings. While the Habs bowed to the New York Rangers in the first round of the 1996 playoffs, there were high hopes for the future of the club. Rookie defenceman David Wilkie displayed strong rushing skills and a superb shot, while Finnish centre Saku Koivu showed unexpected toughness to complement his abundant offensive talents. Coach Mario Tremblay fired back at critics of team captain Pierre Turgeon. "Pierre's an excellent leader," said Tremblay. "A great captain."

Pierre Mondou, director of scouting, says the Habs made mistakes in the past at draft time because "we didn't give small players (like Koivu) and Europeans the benefit of the doubt. That's going to change."

Hockey writer Al Strachan has an interesting theory to explain the Canadiens' tumultuous 1995–96 season. He maintains that Corey had specific plans to make over the Habs before the team moved into the new

Molson Centre. The Roy trade was not a mistake; Corey wanted him out of Montreal. Serge Savard and Jacques Demers? Their dismissals weren't done on a whim. Corey wanted them removed. The three captains who were sent packing in the past couple of seasons? All part of the plan. "Has there ever been a Stanley Cup winner (1993)," asks Strachan, "that has been so ruthlessly dismantled in so short a time?"

Patrick Roy says the years he spent in Montreal with the Habs will always be very special to him. At a press conference in Montreal two days after his angry confrontation with new coach Mario Tremblay, he was apologetic. "I made a mistake," he admitted, "a serious mistake and I apologize to my fans, I hope they will forgive me. I want to thank everybody who believed in me, particularly Ronald Corey who always supported me through tough times. Montreal is a great organization with a lot of class."

He offered no apology to the duo of Tremblay and Houle.

On the previous day, Roy donated $500,000 to McDonald House.

In June he skated off with his third Stanley Cup.

Shutt Speaks Out

In early 1984 coach Bob Berry was again fingered as the cause of a string of dismal performances by the Canadiens. Twelve-year veteran Steve Shutt tore the name off his sweater and threw the jersey into a garbage can after a game in Los Angeles, an outrageous act for any Canadien. It was the ultimate display of frustration and resentment aimed at the coach. When asked about the team's psychological problems under Berry, Shutt said, "We're really down—very frustrated. You play how you practise. You have to be intense. We aren't and that's the reason we've been losing."

Shutt was asked if *Les Glorieux* would ever regain the winning ways of the past.

"With Scotty Bowman," he replied, "what held this team together was our total fear of losing and because we all hated Scotty so much. I wouldn't have done what I did [throw the jersey in the can] if I didn't care. Those seasons we lost only eight or ten games, we'd go into mourning if we didn't win a game. Now the younger guys want to win but they don't know how.

"When we were winning we had a lot of guys with heart. There's still a lot of potential for this team, but if you're playing with a .500 team and you take each loss personally, you'll wind up in the nuthouse. As for the Canadiens' mystique, well, what is that really—the mystique never won any games for us."

Lucky to Be Alive

At the peak of his career, few NHLers could match Guy Lafleur for speed, whether it was on the ice or on the highway. On the ice he was bullet-fast. Away from the Forum, behind the wheel of a high-powered car, he could travel from Montreal to Quebec City at a pace that threatened to leave daylight between the vehicle and its shadow.

In the early morning hours of March 24, 1981, after partying in downtown Montreal, Guy was barrelling along the highway, toward his West Island home, when he fell asleep at the wheel. His car left the road and crashed through a metal fence. One of the fence poles flew up and fractured the car's windshield. Like some tribal spear, it sailed straight toward Guy's head, missing his skull by a fraction of an inch and slicing off part of his right ear.

Lafleur was rushed to hospital, where a plastic surgeon repaired the damaged ear. Police investigators told Lafleur he was extremely fortunate not to have suffered more than a severed ear. If his head had been tilted slightly to the right, they said, the metal pole would have pierced his skull and killed him instantly.

The accident triggered lengthy discussions about Guy's private life. There was talk about his penchant for life in the fast lane and about his sobriety on the night of the accident. Some people said his driving habits were atrocious, but whenever he was stopped by police, a gentle admonishment or warning was the usual result. What's a cop to do when he recognizes Guy Lafleur behind the wheel? One does not ticket the Flower. One would sooner ticket the Pope.

His near-fatal experience appeared to bring Guy to his senses. "I know how lucky I was," he said. "And I think there was a message for me in all of this—one I should heed."

Remember Steve Penney?

Thirteen years after Ken Dryden backstopped the Canadiens to a surprise playoff upset of Boston in the Stanley Cup quarterfinals of 1971, history repeated itself as Steve Penney, another obscure netminder, performed brilliantly in a three-game sweep of the Bruins.

The Canadiens were floundering through their worst season in 40 years, with their two goaltenders, Rick Wamsley and Richard Sevigny, shouldering most of the blame for the team's woes.

In desperation, Sam Pollock turned to Penney, a native of St. Foy, Quebec. Penney had fought his way up from the Flint Generals of the International League to Montreal's American Hockey League farm club in Nova Scotia. Now he'd get a shot at the big time.

At the outset, Penney was hardly a Dryden clone. He lost his first four starts, whereas Dryden won his first six games as a Hab. But Penney caught fire in the playoffs. He led Montreal to a three-game victory over the Bruins in the Adams Division semifinal and was equally successful in a follow-up six-game series against Quebec. Even though the Islanders prevented the

Habs from reaching the Stanley Cup finals that year, Penney had gained hero status with fans and the media. He recorded nine wins and three shutouts in 15 playoff starts. His goals-against average was a sparkling 2.20 and in 1985 he was named to the all-rookie team. Writer Stan Fischler predicted that by the following year Penney would be a better goalie than Dryden ever was.

Where was Penney in 1986? He was home watching the Stanley Cup finals on television, nursing a tender knee. Another obscure puckstopper won rave reviews when Montreal captured the Cup for the 23rd time in Calgary that year. Young Patrick Roy had pushed Penney back into the shadows and his NHL career was virtually over. He'd even been replaced by veteran Doug Soetaert as Montreal's backup goaltender.

At the end of the 1986 season, Montreal swapped Penney to the Winnipeg Jets for goalie Brian Hayward. Penney played in only seven games as a Jet in 1986–87, recorded a goals-against average of 4.59, and was outshone by two youngsters, Pokey Reddick and Daniel Berthiaume. Nobody ever again called him another Dryden. The following season, his last in the NHL, his goals-against average soared to 4.68. In five NHL seasons, Penney compiled a record of 35-38-12 and a goals-against average of 3.62. He was 30-32-10 with Montreal and would be long forgotten but for his spectacular play in the playoffs of 1984.

Canadiens of '84 a Different Breed

Flying Frenchmen indeed!

That's what the fans were saying about *Les Glorieux* in 1984. The players cavorting in blue, white, and red uniforms at the Forum were a different breed than their predecessors.

A melting pot of talent produced a full-blooded Algonquin, a civil engineer, a muscular behemoth who hadn't played in five years, a truck driver turned goaltender, a football linebacker, a pipsqueak from Scandinavia, and a beachboy from San Diego.

Can you name all of the above? Can you name any of the above?

The Algonquin was centre John Chabot, who declined to have his name pronounced in the French manner, Sha-BOW. "It's always been Cha-BOT and it'll stay Cha-BOT," he said.

The civil engineer was left winger Mike McPhee, a graduate of Rensselaer Polytechnic Institute in Troy, New York.

The muscular behemoth—actually he was no longer a behemoth when he joined the club, having shed 35 of his 240 pounds—was bodybuilder Normand Baron, who carried the title Mr. Montreal. Baron hadn't played in five seasons but after seeing Guy Lafleur being pummelled one night, asked for a tryout. He was told to lose 35 pounds and he'd get his chance. To everyone's surprise, Baron shed the weight, proved he could skate like a pro, and was signed to a contract. He wound up playing part of one season in Montreal and part of another in St. Louis. He scored two goals in 27 NHL games before disappearing from the hockey limelight.

The truck driver turned goaltender was 23-year-old Steve Penney, who was called up from the International League and stayed with the Habs for two seasons. Penney was traded to Winnipeg for Brian Hayward in 1986.

The pint-sized Scandinavian was Mats Naslund, a left winger who was drafted 37th overall (second round) by Montreal in 1979. He played eight seasons with the Habs and averaged almost a point a game: 612 points in 617 games. He became a darling of the fans because of his skills and determination—another good little man who played superbly against the biggest and the best. Shades of Henri Richard.

The football linebacker was Craig Ludwig, a Wisconsin native who decided that football had too many practices and not enough games. He switched to hockey, played on an NCAA championship team at Wisconsin (as a walk-on), and graduated to the Canadiens, where he was a member of the '86 Cup-winning team.

The beachboy was Chris Chelios, a Chicago native who grew up in San Diego where surfboards are rampant. Chris moved to Canada to hone his hockey skills, was drafted by Montreal in 1981, and played college hockey at Wisconsin and on the U.S. Olympic team before joining the Habs, where he displayed enormous potential. Off the ice he created some problems. In time, his refusal to conform would lead to his departure for Chicago, where he would mature into one of the greatest defencemen in the game.

Chelios Had to Go

When Serge Savard was fired as general manager of the Montreal Canadiens four games into the 1995–96 NHL season, a reporter asked him about one of his most controversial deals, the 1990 swap of All-Star defenceman Chris Chelios plus a draft choice to Chicago in return for an aging Denis Savard.

GM Savard told *Hockey Night in Canada*'s Ron Maclean, "Chelios had to go. He could not play for Montreal any longer."

Savard confirmed what many close to the Canadiens knew all along, that Corey and the owners of the Canadiens were fed up with the public image projected by Chelios. His off-ice actions were a reflection on the team and Savard was told to get rid of him, even if he failed to get much in return.

For more than a decade, the Canadiens had been reminded that they had selected Doug Wickenheiser over the more popular Denis Savard in the 1980 entry draft. Even though he knew the deal was slanted in favour of the Blackhawks, Serge Savard acquired Denis Savard for Chelios and a second-round draft pick, Michael Pomichter.

By the time Denis Savard joined the Canadiens, his best years (seven straight seasons with 90 points or more) were well behind him. Chelios performed brilliantly for the Blackhawks, setting several club records, being named to several All-Star teams, and winning a second Norris Trophy in 1993.

Memories of Roy

Dick Irvin and I were huddled over our bowls of hot soup in the Texan Restaurant across from the Montreal Forum. This was early in the 1984–85 season, as I recall. Directly across from us, alone in a booth, sat a scrawny, pasty-faced teenager. He'd never have drawn a second glance if Dick hadn't nudged me and whispered, "See that kid over there? They tell me he could be the next great goalie with the Canadiens. Name's Patrick Roy." Dick pronounced it Roy as in Royal.

I took another look. That gawky kid? Looked like a busboy. The next Plante...or Dryden? Hard to believe. How come I'd never heard of him?

I looked up his record and it offered no clues to future greatness. Three years of junior hockey with Granby, where he gave up four to six goals a game on average. Drafted by Montreal in the third round of the 1984 entry draft, 51st overall, Roy was brought up and played 20 minutes of one game late in the season. He performed rather well, allowing no goals (on two shots by Winnipeg), but failed even to get a mention in the *Hockey News*.

When the Canadiens were eliminated from the playoffs (by Quebec) in 1985, Roy's name surfaced again, in a report filed by Glenn Cole of the *Hockey News*. Cole predicted that Roy would supplant both Steve Penney and Doug Soetaert the following year. And that's pretty much what happened. Roy impressed at training camp, played in 47 games, and let the English media know how to pronounce his name. He not only made the all-rookie team with a 23-18-3 mark in regular season play but he caught fire in the playoffs, performing in 20 games and winning all but five. His stinginess earned him a 1.92 goals-against average and the Conn Smythe Trophy as playoff MVP after the Canadiens triumphed over the Calgary Flames.

Skrudland Quick on the Trigger

In game two of the 1986 Stanley Cup Finals, played at the Saddledome in Calgary, the Flames and the Canadiens fought to a 2–2 tie at the end of regulation time.

Many of the fans left their seats for refreshments, while others heeded the call of nature during the intermission. All were anxious to witness the excitement of the overtime period, but hundreds, if not thousands, of spectators were still not back in their seats when the extra frame began. From the faceoff, Montreal controlled the play. The puck wound up on the stick of Brian Skrudland, who scored the winning goal after just nine seconds of play. Ironically, Skrudland was once deemed "too slow" for Canada's national hockey team, much less the swift Canadiens. His was the fastest overtime goal in the long history of the Stanley Cup playoffs.

While Skrudland was being mobbed by his mates, hundreds of Calgarians trooping down the aisles turned in disgust and retraced their steps. Dozens more were still flushing toilets or waiting at the concession stands. They could only ask, "What happened?" The win was the first of four straight for the Habs en route to their 23rd Stanley Cup title.

Six years later, in 1993, overtime wins for Montreal would become commonplace in the playoffs. It was almost as if coach Jacques Demers and his players were destined to win the contests that required extra playing time.

The Habs began the '93 playoffs with an overtime loss to Quebec. Then they won two overtime encounters over the Nordiques and followed up with three overtime victories over Buffalo in a four-game sweep. They added two more in a third series with the Islanders (4–1 Canadiens) and in the finals captured three contests in overtime during a five-game series against the Kings.

The Habs' record of ten straight overtime wins in one playoff year is not likely to be broken in the foreseeable future.

An Outrageous Spectacle

The intimidation factor has long been a part of hockey. The verbal threats, the stick slash at a wrist or ankle, an elbow in the kisser, each occur in almost every game. Sometimes these abrasive tactics give a player or a team a slight edge over the opposition.

But blatant acts of intimidation before a game, while not unheard of, are seldom witnessed. That's why fans and officials used words like "appalled" and "disgusted" to describe a bizarre pregame brawl they witnessed between the Philadelphia Flyers and the Montreal Canadiens at the Forum on May 14, 1987. The donnybrook resulted in a police investigation of the incident, a playoff suspension to the instigator, and fines amounting to $24,000.

It all began innocently enough. Over the course of the season, the Habs had developed a harmless pregame ritual. After the warm-up session, when the opposing team had left the ice, either Shane Corson or Claude Lemieux would shoot a puck into the opponent's net. Most teams weren't even aware of the unconventional ritual. Opponents who were aware of it merely shrugged and called it an "act for children."

After the warm-up period prior to the sixth game of the Conference Final, Corson and Lemieux headed toward the empty Philadelphia net, when they were spotted by Flyer tough guy Ed Hospodar and backup goalie Chico Resch. Harmless ritual or not, the visiting players bristled at the thought of giving up a "goal" before the game even started. Both Flyers leaped onto the ice. Hospodar hooked Corson from behind while Resch threw his goal stick at the puck. Then Hospodar attacked Lemieux. Within seconds players from both teams raced from their dressing rooms to the rink and began flailing away at each other. It was an ugly scene that lasted for about ten minutes and held up the start of the game.

While Montreal police began an investigation of the affair, the following day NHL vice-president Brian O'Neill assessed fines to the culprits totalling $24,500. He also suspended Hospodar for the remainder of the playoffs. The Flyers won the game that night, eliminating the Habs from the playoffs. Afterwards, 38-year-old Chico Resch said, "What we did was wrong. I threw my stick to stop them from putting the puck in our net. We shouldn't have lost our cool. But people who drive cars shouldn't lose their temper when someone cuts them off on the highway. Still, it happens."

TV commentator Don Cherry wasn't surprised the brawl took place. He told me once, "When I coached the Bruins we almost got involved in a punch-out with the Red Wings at the morning skate of all things. We were due to go on the ice at a certain time and half a dozen Red Wings were out there skating around—after their time was up. My guys were getting more ticked off every minute and finally they jumped on the ice and started firing pucks at the Red Wing players. The Wings hustled off the ice when they saw how mad my guys were. You don't fool around with guys like Cashman, Jonathan, and O'Reilly. But it was close. There could have been a major brawl out there at any second."

Gallivan Was a National Treasure

He never played a game for the Montreal Canadiens. And he entered the Habs' dressing room only twice in his life. Yet he became as beloved as the Rocket or Beliveau, as synonymous with hockey excellence as either of those legends.

He was Danny Gallivan, for three decades the voice of the Montreal Canadiens. When he died in his sleep on a February night in 1993 at the age of 75, a nation mourned.

I knew him well, worked with him often, and admired him tremendously. He was lively and charming, generous and kind, humorous and bright. It was always an honour to share a cab ride, a meal, a golf game, or a broadcast booth with one of the greatest broadcasters of this century. He would often talk about his Maritime roots and hockey players with fascinating names, like "Pickles" McNichol and "Leaky" Boates.

Those who penned his obituaries, and there were many, summed up the impact he had on his multitude of listeners.

Al Strachan, writing in the *Globe and Mail*, said,

Gallivan was the man adults looked to for insights and that children listened to on thrillingly late Saturday nights, memorizing his phrases and learning to imitate his inflections that rose and fell like the wail of the Forum's siren.

He never forgot that it was the game, not the trappings that surrounded it, that provided the source of everyone's interest. And he had a passionate love for the game, always defending it against those who saw it only as a source of income.

Eventually the changing times did Gallivan in. The league's power base moved to New York, and Toronto became the media center. The Hockey Night in Canada *people will pay tribute to Danny and pretend that there was never anything but happiness between them. The fact of the matter however, is that Gallivan was not part of the Toronto broadcasting mafia. He challenged their corporate assumptions. As a result, they bounced him from the playoffs in the mid-seventies, making the excuse that if the Canadiens weren't involved, Gallivan shouldn't be either. He was deeply hurt by that, though he never complained publicly. But the news got out and many fans were incensed. In Toronto,* Hockey Night in Canada *executives like Ted Hough shrugged it off. There was no major uproar in Toronto, so Gallivan's axing couldn't have mattered much. Eventually, tired of being treated like a pariah by the* Hockey Night *head office, Gallivan retired to a life of golf and speaking engagements.*

Montreal columnist and broadcaster Ted Blackman, a huge Gallivan supporter, said, "I'll never forgive the people who didn't let Danny broadcast at least half the games in the famous Team Canada–Soviet series in 1972. He deserved to be there. Instead they gave the whole thing to Foster Hewitt."

Ask any of us who spent time in the booth with him our favourite Gallivan anecdote and surely one of us would mention the story of the dead microphone. Danny, you see, loved to speak into a microphone he could hold, a long, cigar-shaped mike he held directly in front of his mouth. When he looked left or right following the action on the ice, he would move the microphone accordingly.

Sometime in the '70s we were introduced to microphones embedded in our headsets. Danny didn't care much for this technological advance, even though it left his hands free. He balked at wearing the headset and insisted on using his old-fashioned mike.

A compromise was reached. Gallivan would wear the headset, through which he would hear important messages from the producer and director, and his voice would travel through the headset mike, but he would keep his hand mike—even though it wasn't plugged in!

And that's the way he carried on. And if the voices he heard from the truck (the production centre) distracted him, or annoyed him, he would simply turn the volume down on his headset and cut them off. One night he and Dick Irvin were discussing a situation and Danny said, "Well, Dick, Ron Andrews, the NHL statistician, is sitting right next to me. He'll know the answer to that question." Danny pushed his hand microphone, the dead one, in Andrews's direction and asked the question. But nobody heard Andrews's reply. He was chatting into an unplugged mike.

Whenever that story was told, as it often was, Danny would be the first to laugh. He was such a good-natured individual, full of Irish wit and humour.

Dick Irvin, who toiled in the booth next to Danny as a colour commentator for many years, a man who faced the daunting task of replacing Gallivan as the Habs' play-by-play voice, said, "It's absolutely amazing the impact Danny had on the country. Even now, nine years after he retired from broadcasting games at the Forum."

Former NHL referee Red Storey, a frequent partner of Gallivan's on the banquet circuit, talked of Danny's penchant for creating colourful phrases, like "Savardian spinnerama" and "cannonading shot."

"Danny got a letter from a university professor one day," said Storey. "The guy told Danny there was no such word as cannonading. Danny wrote back, answering him in three words 'There is now.'"

During his illustrious career, Gallivan broadcast close to 2,000 games, including 16 Stanley Cup wins by the Canadiens.

He grew up in Sydney, Nova Scotia, the son of a coal shipper, one of 13 children in a strict Roman Catholic family. As a teenager he excelled at baseball and was invited to a training camp for the New York Giants. But he injured his arm, ending his dreams of a major-league career. He turned to sports broadcasting and in 1950 he "lucked into" a job covering Montreal games when regular announcer Doug Smith became ill.

When Gallivan arrived at the Forum to replace Smith, he confessed he'd never seen an NHL game and didn't know any of the opposing players on the ice that night. But he studied their photos and memorized the numbers they wore, and everyone was pleased with his presentation. Two years later, when Smith moved to football, Gallivan became a fixture on the broadcasts.

He often talked of great Montreal teams and players, like the Habs of the late '50s, and Rocket Richard: "Those teams played the game in spectacular fashion—with speed and great execution. And the greatest of them all was the 1959–60 edition of the Canadiens. They finished in first place by a wide margin and then swept the Stanley Cup in eight straight games. That was a fabulous team.

"As for the Rocket, he was the most exciting player I ever saw. He was fantastic! Maybe he wasn't the greatest ever—Bobby Orr gets my vote there—but the Rocket was the most dynamic. He was like baseball's Babe Ruth. When a big goal was needed, Richard would surely score it. And who can forget his tremendous desire—those blazing eyes."

I often think of Gallivan as a trendsetter, one whose style and high standards others in the field attempted (not always successfully) to emulate.

And whenever I hear Danny's friend, Canadian tenor John McDermott, sing "Danny Boy," pleasant memories of a good man come back in a rush.

Dick Irvin had a final thought. "I don't think there will ever be anybody in sports broadcasting who will have the same image as the two greats—Foster Hewitt and Danny Gallivan," he said. "Those two names will always be front and centre."

You've got that right, my friend.

Desjardins Nets Three

On June 3, 1993, Eric Desjardins of the Canadiens became the first defenceman in history to notch a hat trick in the Stanley Cup finals. Desjardins's second goal of the game against the Los Angeles Kings tied the score 2–2. It came after a controversial stick measurement late in the third period that resulted in a Montreal power play. At 18:15 of the period, coach Jacques Demers demanded close scrutiny of Marty McSorley's stick, and when it was found to have an illegal curve in the blade, McSorley drew a minor penalty. While he was off, Desjardins scored the tying goal.

After just 51 seconds of overtime, Desjardins swooped in and scored the winning goal, his third of the game and a final-series record.

A week later the Canadiens captured their 24th Stanley Cup championship, defeating the Kings 4–1 in game five. Goaltender Patrick Roy was awarded the Conn Smythe Trophy as playoff MVP, posting a 16–4 playoff record. The Habs established a new NHL record by winning ten consecutive overtime games during the playoffs, an amazing achievement.

Dream Team Honoured

On Saturday, January 12, 1985, the Canadiens' all-time "dream team" was honoured in a special ceremony at the Montreal Forum. The event coincided with the team's 75th anniversary.

More than 20,000 ballots were tabulated to name the members of the team. The fans selected:

- Goalie Jacques Plante, who played on five straight Stanley Cup winners from 1956 to 1960 and captured seven Vezina Trophies.
- Defenceman Doug Harvey, 11 times an NHL All-Star.
- Defenceman Larry Robinson, twice a winner of the Norris Trophy.
- Centre Jean Beliveau, an extraordinary playmaker and scorer for 18 seasons.
- Left winger Dickie Moore, a fierce competitor and two-time NHL scoring champion in the late 1950s.
- Right winger Maurice Richard, who scored 544 regular-season goals and was the first NHL player to score 50 goals in 50 games.
- Toe Blake, who guided the Habs to eight Stanley Cups in 13 seasons, was named coach of the dream team.

The second team:

- Goalie Ken Dryden
- Defenceman Serge Savard
- Defenceman J. C. Tremblay
- Centre Henri Richard
- Left winger Toe Blake
- Right winger Guy Lafleur
- Coach Scotty Bowman
- Special guest Aurel Joliat, then 83 and the oldest living former Hab.

Savard Waited Years to Touch the Cup

When Denis Savard was a small boy growing up in Pointe Gatineau, Quebec, someone brought the Stanley Cup to the local arena one day and everybody gathered around to admire it.

Denis and his friends stood beside the famous trophy, close enough to read the names of the great hockey stars who'd won it in the past. Someone shouted, "Denis, hold onto the Cup like the Montreal Canadiens do when they win it and I'll take your photo."

Denis shook his head. "No, no," he said. "I cannot touch the Stanley Cup. I don't want to. I don't deserve to touch it. It should only be touched or carried by the players who win it."

At the time, of course, Denis did not think that he would ever get to touch the Cup. Only after he became a star in junior hockey in Montreal did he begin to think there might be a chance. He was the top gun on a line of good friends, pals who'd played together since their minor-hockey days. Incredibly, all three were named Denis and all were born on the same day, February 4, 1961. His linemates were Denis Cyr and Denis Tremblay. No wonder they were branded *Les Trois Denis*. Cyr was drafted by Calgary, while the less-fortunate Tremblay was unclaimed in the 1980 draft.

After a decade of play with the Chicago Blackhawks, and two more seasons with Montreal, Savard began to despair of ever holding the Cup. But it's been said that good things happen to those who are patient, those who are willing to wait for whatever rewards life might provide. At age 32, when Montreal captured the Cup in 1993 (after a third-place finish in their division) by defeating the Los Angeles Kings, Savard happily lifted the Cup for the first time. He had finally earned the right to touch it.

Not Another Riot!

When the Montreal Canadiens captured their 24th Stanley Cup championship on June 9, 1993, at the Forum, the celebration that followed soon turned ugly. Fans rampaged through downtown streets, setting fires, smashing store windows, and looting. Damage to municipal property was estimated at more than $1 million. The four-hour riot was the worst in Montreal's history.

There were reports of 168 injuries, including 49 to police officers who vainly attempted to keep the peace. Over 100 arrests were made during the disturbance and the fire department reported half a dozen cases of arson.

Charges against adults included 21 of participating in a riot, 11 of vandalism, eight of theft, seven of concealing stolen goods, four of assault on a police officer, two of assault with a deadly weapon, one of disturbing the peace, and one of breaching probation.

A total of 92 stores were damaged during the riot and store owners later submitted insurance claims totalling more than $2.5 million.

The City of Montreal also racked up huge overtime bills from police, who were obviously caught unprepared for the orgy of destruction. The city also faced dozens of lawsuits from irate merchants and suffered incalculable bad publicity resulting from the rampage.

Montrealers Dominant in Vezina Trophy Wins

Each year the Vezina Trophy is awarded to "the goalkeeper who is judged to be the best at his position." The judges are the NHL's general managers, and the lucky winner receives $10,000. Two runners-up are named. They receive $6,000 and $4,000. Until a few years ago, the trophy was awarded to the "goalkeeper(s) having played a minimum 25 games for the team with the fewest goals scored against it." The old selection process was no fun. There was no suspense on awards night. Everybody knew who the winner or winners would be. One year three goaltenders shared the Vezina: Canadiens Richard Sevigny, Denis Herron, and Michel Larocque.

A check of the *NHL Guide and Record Book* indicates that 34 Montreal goalies have had their names inscribed on the famous old trophy. George Hainsworth's name is there three times, Bill Durnan's six, and Jacques Plante's seven (six times as a Hab and once as a Blue). Plante won the Vezina five consecutive times from 1956 to 1960—a goaltending record.

Montreal's Charlie Hodge won it in 1964 and shared it with teammate Gump Worsley two years later. Rogie Vachon and Worsley captured it in 1968. In 1973 and 1976, Montreal's Ken Dryden skated off with it, and for the next three seasons he shared it with Michel "Bunny" Larocque. The triple winners (Sevigny, Herron, and Larocque) shared it in 1981. The last Montreal netminder to capture the Vezina was Patrick Roy, who held it three times, in 1989, 1990, and 1992.

Strangely, Montreal goalies have seldom been runners-up. Roy was a runner-up in 1991. Before that, a curious researcher must go all the way back to 1967 to find Charlie Hodge's name. The Habs' Gerry McNeil was runner-up to Terry Sawchuk of Detroit in 1953.

In contrast, Chicago's Glen Hall was runner-up six times. He shared it twice, in 1967 with Denis Dejordy (Chicago) and in 1969 with Jacques Plante (St. Louis).

Hab Rookies Seldom Win the Calder

Names of Montreal rookies have been conspicuously absent from the list of Calder Trophy winners in recent years. It's been almost a quarter of a century since goalie Ken Dryden edged Richard Martin (a 44-goal scorer) of the Buffalo Sabres for the coveted Calder. Montreal's Guy Lafleur wasn't even close in the balloting that season.

Jacques Lemaire came close in 1968, only to be edged by Derek Sanderson of the Bruins. Two Habs vied for the Trophy in 1964, with Jacques Laperriere nosing out John Ferguson. Phil Esposito was eligible that season but scored a mere three goals in 27 games for Chicago.

Bobby Rousseau won it in 1962 (over Boston's Cliff Pennington, who scored a grand total of 17 career goals in over 100 games), Ralph Backstrom in 1959 (over Brewer), and Bernie Geoffrion in 1952 (over Hy Buller of New York).

The first Hab to win the Calder was Johnny Quilty, who scored 18 goals and 34 points in his freshman season, 1940–41. He never matched those totals and within three years he was gone from the NHL.

Rocket Richard made his debut in 1942–43 but broke his ankle after 16 games and saw Gaye Stewart of Toronto win the award. Montreal's Glen Harmon was runner-up.

The Rocket was eligible again the following season. He scored 32 goals in 46 games and no doubt fumed when Toronto's Gus Bodnar captured the award with 22 goals in 50 games. To be fair, Bodnar outpointed Richard 62 to 54. The Rocket didn't even finish second in the voting. Teammate Bill Durnan, the Vezina Trophy winner, was next best to Bodnar in the eyes of the selectors.

Jean Beliveau was the odds-on favourite to win the Calder in 1954 but was often injured. He played in only 44 games, scored 13 goals, and finished behind winner Camille Henry of New York and Earl Reibel of Detroit.

Ralph Backstrom outpolled the Leafs' Carl Brewer in 1959.

The Calder drought began after Dryden's win in 1972. The Habs' Chris Chelios came close in 1985, finishing second to Mario Lemieux.

Non-winners of the Calder find their names linked with many of hockey's greatest stars. Doug Harvey won seven Norris Trophies in eight seasons but didn't get a nod for the rookie award in 1948 (Detroit's Jim McFadden was the winner, Boston's Pete Babando the runner-up), Gordie Howe finished behind both Howie Meeker of the Leafs and Jim Conacher of Detroit in 1947, and Wayne Gretzky, despite registering 51 goals and 137 points in his first NHL season, 1979–80, was ruled ineligible for Calder consideration. The previous season, as an 18-year-old, he'd scored 110 points in the WHA, making him "too experienced" to be considered an NHL rookie.

You Could Look It Up

The Montreal Canadiens are the only NHL team to capture the Stanley Cup in five consecutive seasons (1955–56 to 1959–60). The Habs also compiled a four-year streak (1975–76 to 1978–79) and three stretches of back-to-back triumphs. If you include the pre-NHL years, the Montreal Canadiens have skated off with 24 Stanley Cups—an all-time high for championships among professional sports franchises. Major-league baseball's New York Yankees are second on the list; they've been crowned World Series champions 23 times.

The Habs have a winning percentage in the Stanley Cup playoffs of .613 and in 70 years of NHL play have won 130 playoff series and lost only 85. If one adds Stanley Cup triumphs by Montreal teams other than the Canadiens, the city's dominance in hockey is even more impressive. The Maroons (2), Wanderers (4), Montreal AAA (3), Shamrocks (2), and Victorias (4) brought the Cup to Montreal 15 times.

The total number of Stanley Cup celebrations in the city: 39.

GREAT MOMENTS IN MONTREAL'S HOCKEY HISTORY

1893: A team representing the Montreal Amateur Athletic Association is awarded the Stanley Cup and is required to accept challenges for Lord Stanley's gift to hockey.

1896: After the Winnipeg Vics defeat the Montreal Vics for the Stanley Cup in Montreal, a rematch is arranged for Winnipeg, where the Montrealers, paced by Ernie McLea's three goals (the first playoff hat trick), win 6–5 and return the Cup to Montreal.

1897: Ottawa challenges the Montreal Vics for the Stanley Cup but the visitors lose 15–2 in the opening game of hockey's first best-of-three series. Officials cancel the rest of the series and award the Cup to the Vics.

1900: Harry Trihey, a star of the Montreal Shamrocks, scores seven of his team's ten goals in a three-game series with Winnipeg. The Shamrocks follow up their victory over Winnipeg by defeating a Halifax challenge 10–2 and 11–0.

1901: The Shamrocks and Winnipeg Vics play the first overtime match in Stanley Cup play on Montreal ice.

1906: The Montreal Wanderers score at will over Ottawa in a Stanley Cup match, taking a 9–1 lead into the second game of a two-game, total-goals series. But Ottawa, on home ice, fights back and leads 9–1 late in game two. Then Lester Patrick of the Wanderers scores two dramatic goals and they are crowned champions.

1907: The Wanderers lose the Stanley Cup in a two-game series to Kenora, Ontario, the smallest centre ever to claim the Cup. Two months later, the Wanderers win back the trophy from Kenora.

1908: The Wanderers' Ernie Russell scores ten goals in a 22–4 playoff romp over the abysmal Ottawa Vics. The Wanderers of 1908 also defeat Winnipeg, Toronto, and Edmonton (a team of ringers) to retain the Cup.

1910: The National Hockey Association is founded at a meeting in Montreal. Two Montreal clubs, the Wanderers and a new club called *Les Canadiens*, are among the five franchise-holders.

1916: The Montreal Canadiens defeat the Portland Rosebuds in a Cup series played in Montreal. It marks the first time a U.S. team has been allowed to challenge for the trophy.

1917: In November, the National Hockey League is established in a Montreal hotel room. Two Montreal teams, the Wanderers and Canadiens, are charter members. The Canadiens win their home opener 7–4 over Ottawa. Joe Malone collects five goals in the game.

1919: The Canadiens meet the Seattle Metropolitans for the Cup in the second Stanley Cup competition played outside Canada. (The 1917 Cup final was also played in Seattle.) With Montreal tied with Seattle after five games (one game was undecided after 20 minutes of overtime), the flu epidemic hits players from both teams and the series is abandoned. Montreal star Joe Hall later dies of the disease in a Seattle hospital.

1920: The Canadiens set an NHL record for most goals in a game with a 16–3 thrashing of Quebec.

1924: The Canadiens are challenged for the Cup by two Western opponents, one from Vancouver, the other from Calgary. The Canadiens defeat Vancouver two straight in a best-of-three series, then beat Calgary in two games to earn the title "World Champions."

1926: The Montreal Maroons win the Stanley Cup over Victoria in the first playoff series at the new Montreal Forum. Goalie Clint Benedict records back-to-back 3–0 shutouts in the first two games, loses game three 3–2, then shuts out Victoria in the final match 2–0.

1928: Ranger manager Lester Patrick, 44, is forced to play goal in a playoff game against the Maroons at the Forum. The white-haired Patrick takes over from Lorne Chabot, his injured netminder. Patrick allows one goal, the Rangers defeat the Maroons in overtime, and the team goes on to capture the Cup in five games.

1929: Canadiens goalie George Hainsworth records 22 shutouts in 44 games, an NHL record that may never be matched.

1930: George Hainsworth, successor to the legendary Georges Vezina, leads the Canadiens to a Stanley Cup triumph over Boston, after the Bruins play a record 23 games without a loss during the regular season.

1931: The Canadiens, paced by Howie Morenz and Aurel Joliat, capture the Stanley Cup over Chicago.

1935: The Montreal Maroons, with goaltender Alex Connell starring, defeat Toronto for the Stanley Cup.

1936: The longest game in NHL history is played at the Forum on March 24–25. The playoff match between Detroit and the Maroons ends after 176 minutes and 30 seconds when Detroit's "Mud" Bruneteau scores the game's only goal.

1937: Howie Morenz fans fill the Forum on March 11 to pay their final respects to the Canadiens' superstar who died at age 35 a few days earlier.

1938: The Maroons fold and the Canadiens pick up several of their top players.

1939: The Canadiens, with a mere ten victories, become the only NHL club to miss the playoffs.

1940: Dick Irvin resigns as Toronto coach and assumes similar duties with the Canadiens. Elmer Lach and Bill Durnan show up at the Canadiens' training camp.

1942: Rookie Maurice Richard plays in 16 games before being injured. Irvin declares, "He'll become the biggest star in hockey."

1943: Goalie Bill Durnan, 29 and untried, plays in 14 straight games before being defeated. Alex Smart joins the Canadiens and scores three goals against Chicago in his first game. He plays in seven more games but scores only two more goals.

1944: The Canadiens lose only five games all season and win the NHL title for the first time since 1931. In the playoffs, they defeat Chicago four straight in the final series, with Richard setting a playoff record with 12 goals in nine games. On March 23, in a semifinal playoff game, Richard scores all five of Montreal's goals in a 5–1 rout of Toronto. The following December, Rocket Richard sets a record with five goals and three assists in a 9–1 romp over Detroit.

1945: Montreal's "Punch Line" of Maurice Richard, Elmer Lach, and Toe Blake finish one-two-three in the individual scoring race. On March 18, against Boston, Richard amazes with his 50th goal in his 50th game.

1946: The Canadiens defeat Boston in five games in the Stanley Cup finals. In the off-season, Frank Selke, 53, joins the Montreal front office, one week after the resignation of manager Tommy Gorman.

1948: Toe Blake, 35, breaks his ankle and the injury ends his career. Elmer Lach, recovering from a fractured skull, wins the scoring crown by one point over the Rangers' Buddy O'Connor.

1950: On January 5, the Canadiens mark their 40th anniversary in hockey. Newsy Lalonde, Jack Laviolette, and Art Bernier, all members of the first Canadiens team, are introduced at centre ice.

1952: In game seven of a semifinal series against Boston, Rocket Richard is crashed to the ice by Leo Labine. Richard receives six stitches to his head and returns to the ice in a groggy state. Even so, he begins a rink-length rush that carries him past four Bruins. Then, warding off a defenceman, he one-hands a shot past goalie Jim Henry.

1953: Veteran Elmer Lach fires the winning goal in overtime over Boston in game five of the Cup finals. Montreal ousts the Bruins 4–1 in games.

1955: Jean Beliveau scores three power-play goals in 44 seconds, prompting the NHL to change a rule. Soon after, penalized players are allowed to return to the ice after a power-play goal against their team. A riot erupts at the Forum on March 17 after NHL president Clarence Campbell suspends Rocket Richard for the 1955 playoffs. Richard's lengthy suspension for punching a linesman during a game in Boston infuriates his fans and costs him the NHL scoring crown. In the off-season, Toe Blake succeeds Dick Irvin as Montreal coach.

1956: The Canadiens record 100 points and win the Stanley Cup in Toe Blake's rookie season as coach.

1957: Rocket Richard scores his 500th goal. The Canadiens breeze to another Cup win, defeating Boston in five games in the finals. Senator Hartland Molson announces that he has bought controlling interest in the Canadian Arena Company.

1958: Dickie Moore plays the last five weeks of the season with a cast on his wrist and still wins the NHL scoring crown. In the playoffs, the Canadiens beat Detroit and Boston to win their third straight Stanley Cup.

1959: Jacques Plante decides to wear a face mask. Toe Blake becomes the first NHL coach to guide his team to four Stanley Cup championships in a row.

1960: Blake's Canadiens win their fifth straight Cup with a record-tying eight consecutive playoff victories. In September, Rocket Richard retires.

1961: On March 16, Bernie Geoffrion scores his 50th goal to tie the mark of teammate Rocket Richard.

1964: Frank Selke is succeeded as general manager by Sam Pollock.

1965: Montreal defeats Chicago to win the Stanley Cup. Jean Beliveau becomes the first winner of the Conn Smythe Trophy as playoff MVP.

1966: Montreal defeats Detroit to win the Cup in six games. Henri Richard scores a disputed goal to end the final series.

1968: Jean Beliveau becomes the first Montreal player to score 1,000 points. After Montreal wins the Stanley Cup, defeating the St. Louis Blues in four straight games in the finals, Toe Blake retires as coach.

1969: John Ferguson scores the winning goal in the final game as the Canadiens defeat the Blues four games to none in the finals for the Stanley Cup.

1971: Rookie Ken Dryden shines as Montreal ousts Boston in the playoffs. The Canadiens move on to defeat Minnesota and Chicago to capture the Cup. Jean Beliveau retires after 18 seasons. The Canadiens are sold to the Bronfmans and the Bank of Nova Scotia for a reported $15.4 million. Scotty Bowman is hired to coach the team.

1972: The first game in an eight-game series between Team Canada and the Soviet Union is played at the Forum. Canadians are shocked when the poorly equipped visitors crush the cream of the NHL crop 7–3 in game one.

1973: Frank Mahovlich is honoured at the Forum for bettering Jean Beliveau's 507 career goals. Montreal's Yvan Cournoyer wins the Conn Smythe Trophy after the Canadiens capture the Stanley Cup with a six-game victory over Chicago in the finals.

1975: On New Year's Eve, the Canadiens and the touring Soviet Red Army team play a spectacular game at the Forum. The hero of the 3–3 tie is Soviet goaltender Vladislav Tretiak.

1976: The Canadiens require just 13 games to win the Stanley Cup. They oust the defending champion Flyers in four straight games in the finals.

1978: New York goalie Hardy Astrom, playing in his first NHL game on February 25, ends Montreal's unbeaten streak (23-0-5). Guy Lafleur wins his third straight scoring title and the Canadiens sweep to their third straight Cup, defeating Boston in six games in the finals.

1979: On May 10, Guy Lafleur scores a dramatic goal, perhaps the most famous one of his career, enabling Montreal to tie Boston in game seven of a playoff series while Don Cherry's Bruins are killing a too-many-men-on-the-ice penalty. The Canadiens win the game in overtime and go on to defeat the Rangers and capture the Stanley Cup. Bob Gainey is named playoff MVP.

1980: Guy Lafleur becomes the youngest player in history to top 400 career goals. Montreal centre Pierre Larouche becomes the first player in NHL history to score 50 goals with two teams.

1981: Guy Lafleur becomes the quickest 1,000-point scorer in NHL history. The 29-year-old sets the mark in his 720th game.

1983: Serge Savard is hired as the Canadiens' new managing director. Savard reappoints Bob Berry as coach, after Berry was fired from the job 38 days earlier. Savard drafts Soviet goaltender Vladislav Tretiak and agrees to pay Soviet hockey $500,000 for his release, but Tretiak does not report.

1984: Danny Gallivan, the voice of the Canadiens on *Hockey Night in Canada*, retires. On November 26, Guy Lafleur, 33, retires, just 26 goals shy of Rocket Richard's team record of 544 goals.

1985: Jacques Lemaire steps down as Montreal coach and is replaced by college coach Jean Perron.

1986: Larry Robinson, playing in his 1,000th game, is the third Canadien to reach that plateau. The Canadiens win their 23rd Stanley Cup, defeating Calgary in the finals, and set a pro sports record for most playoff titles. A riot breaks out in Montreal following the victory.

1987: The Flyers and the Canadiens engage in a bizarre pregame brawl at the Forum. NHL executive vice-president Brian O'Neill assesses fines totalling $24,500 to the players involved.

1988: The Bruins, losers of 18 consecutive playoff series to Montreal, finally snap the jinx and eliminate the Canadiens in the Adams Division finals. Jean Perron resigns as Montreal coach, citing "pressures from within, including player criticism" as the reason. He is replaced by ex-detective Pat Burns.

1989: The Calgary Flames become the only visiting team to win the Stanley Cup on Forum ice, defeating the Canadiens in game six of the finals.

1993: On June 3, down 1–0 in games and trailing the Los Angeles Kings by a goal in game two in the Cup finals, Montreal calls a successful stick measurement on Marty McSorley. The Canadiens rally, win the game on a record-tying three-goal effort by defenceman Eric Desjardins, and capture their 24th Stanley Cup. The team wins a record ten playoff games in overtime.

1995: On October 16, Ron Corey fires general manager Serge Savard and coach Jacques Demers, replacing them four days later with two surprise appointments, Rejean Houle and Mario Tremblay. On December 2, goaltender Patrick Roy becomes incensed when coach Tremblay leaves him in goal for nine Detroit goals during an 11–1 drubbing, confronts team president Corey, and vows he'll never play for Montreal again. Within days, Roy is traded to Colorado.

1996: On March 2, after 3,228 games and 72 seasons, the last hockey game is played at the Montreal Forum. Montreal beats Dallas 4–1. A few days later, the Canadiens move into the multi-million-dollar Molson Centre.